Thrums from Weavers' Kitchens

A cookbook from the Seattle Weavers' Guild

ISBN 089716-417-2

Editor: Gloria B. Skovronsky
Book Design: Cyndi White
Cover & Illustrations: Nancy Nelson
Graphics: Molly Petram

PEANUT BUTTER
PUBLISHING

Published by Peanut Butter Publishing
200 Second Avenue West
Seattle, WA 98119
(206) 281-5965

First printing September 1992
Printed in Canada

This manuscript was set in Times Roman.
Photos and graphics were digitally scanned
on IBM and Macintosh personal computers.

Dedicated to the WEAVERS - they spin, dye, sew, knit, design, garden . . . and COOK! They add flair and flavor to life.

What are THRUMS?

Thrums are the remaining unwoven threads left at the beginning and the end of a woven fabric when it is removed from the loom. We may think of them as waste, or we may look on them as the connection between the old and the new. Often we use our thrums to plan new projects, or save them for dye samples. The careful weaver will keep a record of everything that goes into each project. These "ingredients" may include an idea or inspiration, samples, the draft or pattern, woven amounts of materials, finishing techniques, and often a critique of the project itself. Usually a few thrums are included as part of the record. In this way the thrums become part of the recipe that connects us to each woven piece of cloth.

This project would not have been possible without the help of three young computer wizards who pushed us, not always gently, into the 21st century world of desk top publishing: Shannan Cummings, who typeset and printed the manuscript through countless revisions, Jason Knoefler, who produced a perfectly formatted union of text and graphics and Sarah Skovronsky, who effortlessly transferred files from system to system as our ideas outstripped our equipment. These people juggled several balls in the air at the same time and, with their energy and good humor, never let a one drop.

We are grateful to The Weaving Works, Seattle, which provided the use of computer equipment, and to Cottage Weaving, Issaquah, which supplied woven samples for the use of our illustrator.

Our thanks also to Elliot Wolf, our publisher; Bill Wickett, our photographer; Joe Miller, who provided our mannequin; and last but not least to Nancy Nelson, whose beautiful and expressive line drawings perfectly represented our desire to marry good weaving with good food.

Introduction

As weavers, we remain closely connected to the earth and all natural things. Many of us raise our own sheep, gather basketry and dye materials and, of course, nurture gardens which provide an array of edibles, flowers and a welcome outlet to exercize muscles tired from hours at the loom. We thrive on PROCESS -- we like to make things from start to finish whether it be the weaving of beautiful cloth or the preparation of delicious food. We also love to share, which is why we have enjoyed every moment of the taste-testing, of the new cooking methods, of the wealth of memories which have been ours to savour for the past few months. We found that most of the recipes in this book are simple, quick to prepare, and destined to become valued additions to lists of meals we enjoy most often.

We wish to honor all of the Seattle Weavers' Guild members who gave us their treasured recipes, many of which have been handed down from generation to generation and are published here for the first time. We hope you enjoy them as much as we have.

Sue Bichsel   Rhonda Goldsmith

Roberta Loves   Josie Utley

Molly Pelram   Cyndi White

Gloria B. Skovronsky   jean wilson

The love of weaving and the desire to preserve it within our culture became the bonds that drew a small group of women together in Seattle, Washington in 1936. After many meetings and much planning the Seattle Weavers' Guild was formally established on January 23, 1937. Our "Founding Mothers" had the right ideas, setting workable and lasting policies and goals that remain viable today after fifty-five years.

Our membership began to grow from 12 to 21 members, to 70 in 1939, to over 350 today. A true guild, members have always shared ideas and expertise through meetings, study groups, and programs from those early days to the present. As our membership grew, so did our widening interest in all phases of the fiber arts: spinning, dyeing, basketry, papermaking, historical, modern and ethnic textiles, color and design, garments, rugs and tapestries, and weaving for the home and for industry.

And as our interests multiplied, we continued to expand the scope of our programs. Our annual bazaars (now sales), first held in 1938, have become an exciting outlet for our members to introduce their work to the public and to learn marketing and display techniques. We established the beginnings of our now extensive library of over one thousand books and periodicals, many of which are rare and out of print. In 1949 we held our first juried exhibition in the east gallery of the Seattle Art Museum. Since that time, we have had numerous fine exhibits, some co-sponsored, throughout the Puget Sound area. In 1957, our first Bulletin with a weaving sample and fabric swatch was introduced, a tradition which continues to this day. Many Seattle Weavers' Guild members have become internationally known for their textiles, clothing articles and books. We teach at the local level and at national conferences to share our love and knowledge for the fiber arts.

The Guild today is as vibrant and energetic as in those early days in 1937. This year, we participated once again in the renowned Pacific Northwest Arts and Crafts Fair in Bellevue, Washington. We presented a gallery of members' weavings and featured an educational booth where the public could see various fiber demonstrations and also enjoy some hands-on experience.

1992 marks the year that we will publish our first cookbook and in July 1993 we will host the biennial conference of the Association of Northwest Weavers' Guilds. <u>Fiber Fanfare '93</u> will be held at the University of Washington and will feature speakers, workshops, lectures, seminars and exhibits on every phase of the fiber arts. The Seattle Weavers' Guild continues to offer a wide and varied spectrum of activities for the weaving community: internationally known speakers, innovative "mini-workshops" which focus on a particular technique or concept, comprehensive educational workshops, and supportive study groups which provide for the exchange of ideas and close contact among members.

The closeness and camaraderie that we feel as guild members have been translated into more than fifty years of a rich and varied weaving legacy. We all look forward to seeing what the next fifty years will bring.

Table of Contents

APPETIZERS & SIDE DISHES

SOUPS & SALADS

BREADS

THE MAIN COURSE

SWEETS

Appetizers & Side Dishes

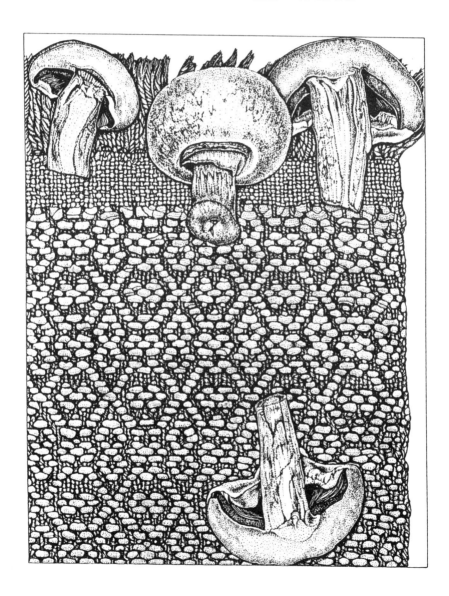

BAKED GARLIC

9-12 heads of garlic
½   cup olive oil
½   cup butter, melted
¼   cup water
     dried herbs of your choice
     toasted baguettes, sliced, or melba
       crackers
     Montrachet cheese (goat cheese)
     (recipe follows)

Preheat oven to 350°F. Peel the loose "paper" off garlic, leaving the
cloves all intact. Cut ¼ inch off the top of each head of garlic (not the
root end). Place heads in a baking pan just large enough to hold the
garlic comfortably with the cut side up. Mix the oil, butter and water
and pour over garlic. Sprinkle with any of the following fresh or dried
herbs: rosemary, basil, oregano, thyme, etc. (We find that rosemary
is a must and fresh herbs and lots of them are the best.) Cover tightly
with lid or foil. Bake for 1 hour or until garlic is very soft and
spreadable. (May be baked for 2 hours at 250°.) Serve warm with
thinly sliced toasted baguettes or melba crackers and Montrachet
cheese.

Kate

Kate Lange-McKibben

*Recipe adapted from David McKibben and the
Adriatica Restaurant, Seattle*

MONTRACHET CHEVRÉ
(goat cheese)

1 package goat cheese
¼ cup olive oil
   fresh or dried herbs of your choice

Slice cheese into ½ inch rounds and place in flat bowl. Pour olive oil over. Sprinkle top with herbs: oregano, thyme, basil, and/or tarragon to suit your taste. Cover tightly and marinate for 2-3 hours. Stir cheese carefully every 30 minutes. (If you use a Tupperware style bowl, you can turn over every ½ hour during marinating time.) To serve, spread cheese on baguette or cracker, then spread with 1 or 2 cloves of baked garlic.

Kate

Kate Lange-McKibben

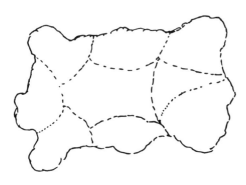

fleece

Kathy Dannerbeck, baskets, woven of cedar bark with Northwest coast Indian techniques, 5" and 2" diameters, 1987; 4½" x 8" x 5", 1990.

Many weavers also enjoy growing their own vegetables. This recipe uses the garden's bounty. I make a large batch, keep it refrigerated and use it as a hearty appetizer, a light dinner or a snack. I've taken it to the SWG Garment Group summer potluck several times.

VEGETABLE CAPONATA

1 large tomato
1 large can stewed tomatoes,
      liquid reserved
½ cup wine vinegar
2 teaspoons sugar
¼ cup olive oil
2 medium eggplants, with stems removed
2 medium zucchini
2 large bell peppers, red or yellow
1 large onion
2 large tomatoes
1 pound mushrooms, fresh
6 ounces green Spanish pimento stuffed
      olives, sliced
   salt
   French bread

Preheat oven to 400°F. In a food processor or blender, puree the tomato, stewed tomatoes, wine vinegar, sugar and olive oil. Cube the eggplants, zucchini, bell peppers, onion, tomatoes and mushrooms. Place cubed vegetables in a very large shallow cooking dish, add the olives and toss with liquid puree mixture. Bake until vegetables are soft (about 2 hours) and all liquid has evaporated, stirring every 20 minutes. (If too soupy, spoon out some of the liquid at the end of the 2 hours). Add salt to taste. Cool and serve with French bread. Can be made ahead and refrigerated up to 1 week. Serves a crowd.

Kathy

Kathy Dannerbeck

LAURA LEE'S HUMMUS

1   15 ounce can garbanzo beans, drained,
        liquid reserved
2   tablespoons olive oil
¼   cup sesame seeds, browned in a dry fry
        pan
3   tablespoons lemon juice
1   clove garlic, crushed
      paprika, black olives, or sesame oil as
        condiment
      pocket bread, cut into 1/8ths

Place beans, olive oil, seeds, lemon juice and garlic into a blender and blend into a paste, adding some of the reserved liquid from the beans to thin mixture a little, if necessary. (It should be thick like peanut butter.) Top with paprika, black olives or sesame oil. Use pocket bread as a scoop to eat. Enjoy!

Marcy

Marcy Johnson

MELTED BRIE IN SOURDOUGH CRUST

1	large round sour dough loaf of bread
1/3	cup olive oil
2	cloves garlic, minced
1-1½	pound round of Brie cheese

Preheat oven to 350°F. With a serrated knife, cut down through top of bread to leave a shell about ½ inch thick on sides. Do not cut through bottom crust. Slide fingers down inside the cut sides of loaf and pull free in a single piece, leaving about a ½ inch thick base in the bread shell. Cut 1½ inch slits around the rim of shell about 1½ inches apart. Cut the removed center bread into slices about 2 X 2½ inch thick.

Place shell and slices onto a 10 X 15 inch shallow baking pan or cookie sheet. Mix oil and garlic in small bowl. Brush inside of shell with about 3 tablespoons oil; brush slices with the remaining oil.

Cut cheese into 2 X 2 inch squares and fill shell. Trim cheese to fit the circle and ease melting. Bake for 10 minutes. Remove bread slices to a rack to cool. Continue baking cheese-filled bread until cheese melts, about 10 minutes longer.

Place cheese-filled crust on a serving plate surrounded with toasted bread slices. Makes 10-12 appetizer servings.

Cyndi

Cyndi White

Sometimes we eat this for dinner with a Caesar salad and a glass of red wine.

CHEESE-CHILI TARTLETS

3   ounces butter, cold, cut in pieces
3   ounces cream cheese
1   cup plus 2 tablespoons all-purpose
    flour
3/4 cup Nokellost or Jack cheese, grated
4   ounces Ortega chilies, chopped
1/3 cup sour cream
1/3 cup mayonnaise
    paprika

Preheat oven to 350°F. For cream cheese pastry: cream butter and cream cheese in food processor with steel blade. Add flour and process until thoroughly combined. Scrape from bowl and cover with plastic wrap; chill dough until fairly firm (1 hour). Form into 1 inch balls and press into mini muffin or tartlet pans. Bring sides up fairly thick so they don't crumble or run over.

Filling: put approximately 1 teaspoon Nokellost cheese, then 1 teaspoon chilies in tart shell. In small bowl, mix sour cream and mayonnaise; top each tartlet with a dollop (1 teaspoon) cream mixture. Sprinkle with paprika. Bake for 25-30 minutes. Serve warm or refrigerate or freeze when cool. Freezes well (reheat on cookie sheet at 350°F for 15 minutes.) Makes 18-20 tartlets.

Alternate filling: use tiny shrimp in place of chilies.

Josie

Josie Utley

The great thing about these little morsels, besides their wonderful taste, is their refreeze-and-reheat ability.

I make 3 or 4 dozen at a time and freeze them in plastic containers. Then on a day when I can't bear to stop weaving but have guests coming I pop some in the oven for 15 minutes and people marvel that I had the time to make them. Great for weaver's potlucks, PTA teas, drop-in visitors. Also convenient when you're planning a big party and need some do ahead hors d'oeuvres, since they don't suffer from freezing and reheating.

A tip: for dessert tartlets, add a little sugar and orange peel or liqueur to the pastry and fill with chess pie (James Beard) or a butter tart filling. Great fun for a work party or cooking class too, rolling and shaping all those little balls while having a good gab-fest.

P.S. You'll want to eat some when they come out of the oven, so make extras.

LAYERED CHEESE TORTA

1 pound cream cheese, room
    temperature
1 pound unsalted butter, room
    temperature
    water
    cheese cloth
    fresh basil leaves
    fillings (recipes follow)
    baguettes, sliced

Beat cream cheese and butter with an electric mixer until very smooth.
Cut cheese cloth into two 18 inch squares and moisten with water;
wring dry. Smoothly line a loaf pan or mold with cheese cloth layers;
drape excess over rim of mold. (If desired, place fresh basil leaves on
top of cheese cloth in an attractive manner.) Spread a layer of cheese
mixture in bottom of mold, evenly, with a spoon. Dot filling mixture
(see below) over cheese, then spread evenly and cover all the cheese.
(You can decide how many layers you want by how much filling you
use each time.) Repeat until mold is filled, finishing with cheese layer.
Fold ends of cheese cloth over top and press down lightly with hands.
Chill until torta feels firm, about 1 hour. Invert onto a serving dish
and gently pull off cheese cloth. (Do not keep cheese cloth on too
long, as it will make the filling bleed onto the cheese.) Serve
immediately, or wrap with plastic wrap. Can be refrigerated up to 5
days. Serve with baguettes.

LAYERED CHEESE TORTA, cont'd.

Fillings:

Pesto: In a food processor, whirl 2½ cups lightly packed fresh basil leaves, 5 ounces freshly grated Parmesan cheese and ½ cup olive oil. Stir in ¼ cup pine nuts, salt and pepper to taste.

Sun-dried tomato: Drain one 10½ ounce can of dried tomatoes in olive oil (reserve 2 tablespoons of oil). Whirl tomatoes with the reserved oil in a food processor until finely chopped.

Cyndi

Cyndi White

I love to entertain and make very special food for my guests. This recipe is really easy AND beautiful to serve. I buy lots of fresh basil in the summer so I can make the pesto and freeze it for use all year. At Christmas, use both fillings for a festive look. Needless to say, this is not a dieter's recipe!

Cyndi White, "Strip Jacket," pink, grey and white cotton, woven in sections, sewn with handspun wool, 1989.

CHEESE PUFFS

1 cup water
½ cup butter or margarine
1 cup all-purpose flour
4 large whole eggs
1 cup Cheddar cheese, grated
½ cup Parmesan cheese, shredded

Preheat over to 400°F. Bring water and margarine to a rolling boil in a saucepan. Stir in the flour all at once. Stir over low heat until the mixture forms a ball. Remove from heat. Add eggs, one at a time, beating each in thoroughly. Mix in cheeses. Drop dough by teaspoons onto ungreased cookie sheet. Bake about 20 minutes until puffed and golden brown. Makes about 60 puffs.

Susan

Susan Snover

This is a great, quick appetizer that leaves you more time to weave.

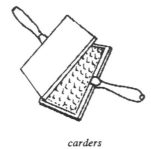

carders

HOT TOM TREAT

1   cube bouillon
1   cup boiling water
1   large can tomato juice
½-1 teaspoon onion salt
     lemon slices

Dissolve bouillon cube in water. Heat with tomato juice to boiling point. Put lemon slices in mugs; pour hot juice over.

Susan

Susan Young

While weaving on a cold wintery day at Alpental, a friend who was shivering from a day of skiing asked, "Do you have...?" Her concoction was such a treat and so easy, I now keep all the necessary ingredients on our boat for those pick-me-up days.

DIED AND GONE TO HEAVEN POTATOES

1   32 ounce package frozen hash brown
       potatoes
2   cups sour cream
1   can cream of chicken or celery soup
½   cup onion, minced or grated
6   ounces sharp Cheddar cheese, grated
1   cup or more corn flakes, crushed
½   cup butter, melted

Preheat oven to 350°F. In a 9 X 13 inch shallow baking pan, combine the potatoes, sour cream, soup, onion and cheese. Spread mixture evenly to fit the pan. Cover with corn flakes and drizzle with melted butter over all. Bake uncovered for 1 hour. Makes 10-12 servings.

Margaret

Margaret Schindler

Best recipes come from friends and two friends gave me this one in the same month. Since then I've discovered it is very popular in the Mid-West.

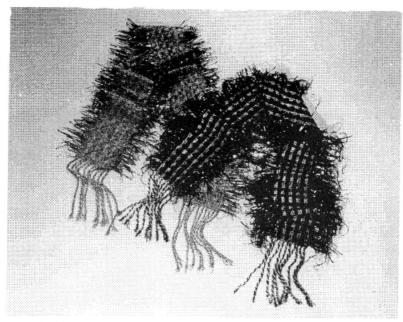

Gloria B. Skovronsky, tinsel scarves, 73" x 78", cotton and rayon, woven in M's and O's with multicolored supplementary mylar strands, 1989.

NANA'S CUCUMBER AND ONIONS

1 cucumber, peeled, about 2½ inches in diameter
1 quart water
¼ cup salt
Brine:
1½ cups apple cider vinegar
1½ cups water
3-4 tablespoons granulated sugar
1 large yellow onion, thinly sliced
  black pepper, cracked

Slice the peeled cucumber into ¼ inch slices and put into a bowl. Mix water and salt and pour over cucumber. Let stand 2-4 hours. To make brine: in medium saucepan, combine vinegar, water, and sugar. Heat to a full rolling boil, then let cool. Drain cucumbers into a colander and dry off in a kitchen towel - don't rinse the cucumber. Layer cucumbers and onions in a small serving bowl. Pour cooled brine over all and top with fresh, cracked black pepper. Best when served within 12 hours. Makes 8-10 appetizer servings.

Gloria

Gloria B. Skovronsky

When my great-grandmother, Johanne Andersen, emigrated from Denmark at the turn of the century, she brought with her two young children and a host of recipes. She opened a boarding house in Council Bluffs, Iowa and my grandmother, Bodil Andreasen, lived there. This side dish satisfies the Danish love of pickled brine. My Nana is an advocate of the "little bit of this, a little bit of that" school of cooking, so adjustments to the brine should be made to your personal taste.

SQUASH CAKES

olive oil for frying
¼ cup Bisquick
2 whole eggs, beaten
½ cup mashed potatoes (can be from
  leftovers)
¼ cup frozen corn or drained canned corn
1 zucchini or other summer squash, medium grated
¼ cup Cheddar cheese, grated
salt and pepper to taste

Heat a heavy griddle until a drop of water dances on surface. Add 1 teaspoon - 1 tablespoon olive oil to barely cover bottom. Just before frying, in a large mixing bowl, mix together Bisquick, eggs, mashed potatoes, corn, zucchini, cheese, salt and pepper. This batter is moist and the squash will release more moisture. If it is too moist, add a little more Bisquick. Fry like small pancakes; serve immediately.

Roberta

Roberta Lowes

We always seem to need new creative ways to use up extra zucchini from the garden. These pancakes make a good lunch dish served with a fresh green salad.

18

A WEAVER'S VEGETABLES

2   tablespoons olive oil
3-4 small zucchini, chopped
1   small onion, diced
4-6 fresh mushrooms, sliced
2-3 Roma or plum tomatoes, chopped
       ground pepper to taste
up to 1 teaspoon favorite herbs to taste
½   teaspoon water

In large frying pan, heat olive oil and saute zucchini, onion, mushrooms and tomatoes for several minutes. Add pepper, herbs and water. Cover, reduce heat to low and continue cooking for about 5 minutes.

Variations and additions - add any of the following: summer squash, green beans, wine or stock instead of water, garlic (especially elephant garlic), toasted almonds, sesame seeds and soy sauce, Parmesan or Romano cheese, onions, or red or yellow peppers.

Ruth

Ruth Beck

For the cook who would rather be weaving, these vegetables make their own sauce so they dress up plain rice, pilaf or potatoes. They also look good over fish and chicken and will wait if the family is late.

Soups & Salads

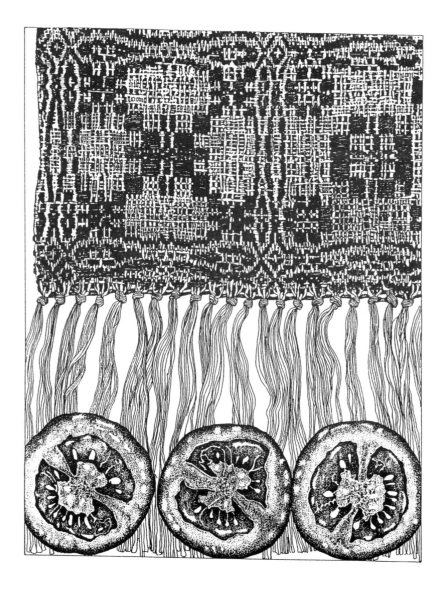

RUSSIAN CABBAGE BORSCHT

1½	cups potatoes, thinly sliced
1	cup fresh beets, thinly sliced
4	cups water or stock
1½	cups onions, chopped
2	tablespoons butter
1	scant teaspoon caraway seeds
2	teaspoons salt
1	stalk celery, chopped
1	large carrot, sliced
3	cups white cabbage, chopped
	black pepper to taste
¼	teaspoon dill weed
1	tablespoon apple cider vinegar, plus
	1 teaspoon apple cider vinegar
1	tablespoon honey, plus 1 teaspoon honey
1	cup tomato puree
1	tablespoon raisins (optional)

Topping:
    sour cream or yoghurt
    dill weed
    tomatoes, chopped

In a medium saucepan, cook potatoes and beets in water or stock until tender, about 10 minutes. Drain, but save the water and set aside. In a large kettle or stock pot, sauté the onions in butter. Add caraway seeds and salt. Cook until onions are translucent, then add celery, carrots and cabbage. Add the water from the potatoes and beets and cook covered until all the vegetables are tender. Add potatoes, beets, pepper, dill weed, vinegar, honey, tomato puree and raisins. Cover and simmer slowly for at least 30 minutes. Serve with sour cream, dill weed and tomatoes. Makes 4-5 servings.

Beth
Beth Zimmerman

Adapted from the Moosehead Cookbook by M. Katzen

COLD BORSCHT

10	large raw beets, peeled or 3 #303 cans beets, liquid reserved
2½	quarts water, 1½ quarts if using canned beets with juice
1	onion, minced
3	garlic cloves, minced or 3 tablespoons garlic powder
4	tablespoons sugar
3-4	tablespoons vinegar juice of 1 lemon
2	whole eggs
1	cup sour cream

Combine beets, water, onion and garlic in sauce pan. Bring to boil and cook over low heat for 1 hour. Add sugar, vinegar and lemon juice. Cook 10 minutes. Remove beet solids and discard. Beat eggs in bowl until frothy. Gradually add eggs to the soup stirring steadily to prevent curdling. Chill 4 hours. Garnish with sour cream. Makes about 2 quarts.

MARIANNE

Marianne Costello

kitchen scale

23

*Molly Petram, afghan, 61" x 46", wool, mohair, and rayon woven in
shades of lavender, 1990.*

**This is a wonderful busy day dinner. Timing is not critical if you get
preoccupied, and it reheats beautifully.**

BAKED BEEF MINESTRONE

2   tablespoons olive or salad oil
1   large onion, sliced
2   pounds lean beef stew meat, cut in bite
      sized pieces
1   cup water
2   cloves garlic, minced
1   cup carrots, sliced
1   cup zucchini, sliced
1   cup celery, sliced
1   small green pepper, seeded and cut into strips
1   15 ounce can tomatoes or 3 fresh, peeled, quartered
3   cups cabbage, shredded
½   teaspoon each granulated sugar,
      rosemary, basil, thyme
¼   teaspoon pepper
3   14 ounce cans beef broth (regular strength)
3   cups cooked small shell macaroni
    Parmesan cheese

Preheat oven to 400°F. Put oil, onion and beef in large casserole. Bake uncovered for 40 minutes, stirring occasionally. Add water, cover, reduce heat to 350°F and cook for 1 hour. Add garlic, carrots, zucchini, celery, green pepper, tomatoes and cabbage. Sprinkle with sugar, rosemary, basil, thyme and pepper. Add the beef broth, cover and bake 1½ hours. Boil water in sauce pan and cook macaroni until al dente, about 8 minutes. To serve, put some hot, cooked macaroni in a bowl. Ladle soup over. Pass the Parmesan cheese. Makes 6 servings

Molly

Molly Petram

MISS RAITT'S FRENCH ONION SOUP

1 tablespoon butter or margarine
1 medium onion, chopped
1 can Campbell's consomme or bouillon soup
1 soup can of water
  Cheddar cheese, grated
  slices of bread, (at least one per person)

Set oven temperature to broil. Melt the butter in a sauce pan. Add onion and sauté until glazed - do not let pieces brown. Add soup and water and heat. Meanwhile, pile cheese on bread slices and melt in oven. Cut bread into crouton sized cubes. Put the croutons into individual bowls and add soup. Serve immediately. Makes 2 servings.

Midge

Midge Dodge

Miss Raitt was the venerable head of the home economics department for whom Raitt Hall on the University of Washington campus was named. She gave a group of dietician interns this recipe in the 1940s. I was privileged to be one of them. This is what to fix after long hours at the loom when you find your cupboard is almost bare.

MYSTERY (ZUCCHINI) SOUP

1   pound zucchini (about 4 cups), sliced
1   small onion, chopped
1   stalk celery, sliced
1-2 tablespoons butter
2   cups chicken broth
½   teaspoon lemon juice
½   teaspoon curry powder, or to taste
      (½ teaspoon is very mild)

Garnish:
    chopped chives
    parsley
    green onion
    sour cream

In stock pot, cook zucchini, onion and celery in butter until softened and translucent, about 12 minutes. Combine broth and lemon juice and curry powder with cooked vegetables. Puree in blender or processor until foamy. Serve hot or chilled, topped with chives, parsley or green onions and a dollop of sour cream, if desired. Makes 4 servings.

Jane

Jane Andrews

I call this "mystery" soup because my guests have never been able to identify the main ingredient. It is quick, easy, delicious and healthy! Add more curry powder for a stronger flavor.

Joanne Croghan, jacket with scarf, black cashmere/wool woven in plain weave; scarf and jacket trim woven in silk, wool, rayon and cotton in twill with supplementary warps, 1992.

PORTUGUESE MAN O'WAR SOUP

1   mild Italian sausage, crumbled
1   hot Italian sausage, crumbled
1   Polish sausage, torn into small pieces
1   pound dried kidney beans (soaked and
        cooked previously) or one 28 ounce can
        kidney beans, drained
1   28 ounce can whole tomatoes, chopped
1   teaspoon each oregano and tarragon, or
        2 teaspoons oregano
    salt and pepper to taste
½   head white cabbage, sliced into strips
1   large onion, chopped
3   carrots, chopped or sliced
    water
    tomato juice if needed

Fry sausages in large stock pot until browned; drain fat. Add beans, tomatoes, salt, pepper, oregano, tarragon, cabbage, onion, carrots and water to cover. Simmer most of the day. Best when made a day ahead. Add tomato juice if too thick. Serve with crusty bread and tossed green salad.

Marilyn

Marilyn Watts

This came to me years ago at a "Soup for Lunch" meeting. You can modify it with less meat and more vegetables but the hot Italian sausage really gives it punch.

PUMPKIN BLACK BEAN SOUP

1	pound black beans, washed, drained
1½	cups onion (3 onions), chopped
3	cloves garlic, minced
3	tablespoons butter or olive oil
3/4	cup canned tomatoes
1	cup canned pumpkin
2½-3½	cups beef stock
4	tablespoons sherry or balsamic vinegar
1-2	tablespoons ground cumin
	salt and pepper to taste
4	tablespoons sherry or balsamic vinegar
6	ounces Polish kielbasa, ham or other smoked sausage
½	cup medium sherry, if desired

In a stock pot, cover beans with boiling water and soak for 3-4 hours. Drain. Cover with water to 2 inches above beans. Simmer partially covered 2-3 hours until tender. Drain liquid and mash or process until chunky. In stock pot, saute onions and garlic in oil until tender. Add beans, tomatoes, pumpkin, 2½ cups stock, vinegar, cumin, salt and pepper to beans. Slice sausage into coin sized pieces; saute until brown; drain fat. Add to beans. Bring soup to a boil and cook 20 minutes or as long as it takes to reduce to desired consistency. Stir frequently. Add extra stock or extra sherry, if desired.

Kay

Kay English

Recipe adapted from <u>Gourmet</u> magazine

This soup can be made very low in fat by omitting the sausage and "sauteing" the onions and garlic in stock instead of fat. Serve the soup in a hollowed out pumpkin with toasted pumpkin seeds on top or with nonfat yoghurt, sour cream, salsa and cilantro as toppings. It can also be served over rice. Freeze and defrost in the microwave for a quick supper.

dyers woad
(Isatis tinctoria)

Roberta Lowes, "Collapse Scarf," 90" X 9", silk, wool, linen and handspun mohair, handpainted in shades of blue, rose and purple, 1992.

When salmon is at a lower price, it is our favorite food! This is a wonderful variation on our Northwest clam chowder. It freezes well, but I would suggest freezing it without the fish for a fresher flavor.

NORTHWEST SALMON CHOWDER

1	onion, chopped
2	medium leeks, chopped (all the white part and most of the tender green leaves)
1	tablespoon olive oil
1	tablespoon all-purpose flour
2	14 ounce cans chicken broth
6-8	medium potatoes, chopped into 1 inch cubes
1	carrot, diced
1	stalk celery, diced
1	teaspoon salt
½	teaspoon pepper
½	teaspoon thyme
2	teaspoons White Wine Worcestershire sauce
1	teaspoon Mrs. Dash spice mixture
1	teaspoon dill
½-1	cup milk or light cream
½	cup frozen green peas
½	cup frozen corn
6	ounces cooked salmon, canned or fresh, separated into chunks

In soup kettle, saute onion and leek in olive oil until limp and translucent. Add flour and stir. Immediately add chicken broth and whisk to keep smooth. Add cut potatoes, carrot, celery salt, pepper, thyme, Worcestershire and Mrs. Dash. Simmer, until vegetables are tender. Reserve 1-2 cups potatoes. Puree remaining potatoes, carrots, celery and seasonings in a blender or food processor. Return to soup kettle. Thin with milk or light cream. Add peas and corn. Cook over lowered heat, just until hot. Add the salmon and reserved potato chunks and serve. Makes 4-6 servings.

Roberta

Roberta Lowes

WARM GRECIAN CHICKEN SALAD

1-2	tablespoons olive oil
¼-½	cup lemon juice
1	tablespoon rosemary
1	teaspoon scallions, chopped (green onion)
1	tablespoon parsley, chopped
½-1	teaspoon crushed red pepper
¼	cup onion, finely chopped
2-3	boneless chicken cutlets
	mixed lettuces, torn in pieces, as desired
	Feta cheese, cut in chunks, as desired
	tomato chunks, as desired
	roasted peppers, diced, as desired
	olives, as desired
2-3	tablespoons boiled Orzo (small pasta shaped like egg)

In boiling water, cook Orzo until al dente, rinse in cold water and drain. In large bowl, mix oil, lemon juice, rosemary, scallions, parsley, red pepper and onions together. Add chicken and marinate for 2 or more hours. In salad bowl, mix lettuce, cheese, tomato, peppers, olives and pasta. Broil chicken (over a flame if possible), and slice into ½ inch wide strips. Serve over salad. Serve with oil and vinegar with perhaps a bit of oregano, salt and pepper. Makes 4 servings.

Kay

Kay English

Recipe adapted from the Museum Cafe, New York City.

IRANIAN SOUP OR SALAD

3   medium cucumbers, peeled
32 ounces plain yoghurt
1   cup walnuts
1   cup raisins
1   cup shallots, leeks or green onions, diced
1   tablespoon dill

For salad: slice cucumbers in half lengthwise and scoop out seeds with a spoon. Slice into ¼-½ inch slices. In a bowl, combine cucumbers with yoghurt, walnuts, raisins, shallots and dill. Chill several hours before serving. Makes 8-12 servings.

For soup: Add 2 cups milk to mixture.

MARIANNE

Marianne Costello

GREEK CHICKEN SALAD

1½   cup cooked skinless chicken breast,
        shredded or cubed
1   cucumber, peeled, seeded and chopped
3/4   cup Feta cheese, crumbled
½   cup sliced ripe olives
¼   cup chopped parsley
¼   cup mayonnaise
½   cup plain yoghurt
1-2 cloves garlic, minced
2   teaspoons dried oregano, crushed

In a large bowl, combine chicken, cucumber, Feta, olives, parsley, mayonnaise, yoghurt, garlic and oregano; toss. Can be served on a bed of lettuce with sliced tomatoes as decorative addition to the plate.

Jean Sullivan

A standard summer supper salad. The recipe came from my mother who found it in a 1985 Better Homes and Gardens. I have changed the proportions according to our taste - one could contrive to "massage" the recipe, keeping the basic ingredients. It is known to cohorts at Weaving Works as "Jean's Mom's Salad".

CHINESE CELERY AND SHRIMP SALAD

Salad:
1   6 ounce can small shrimp
1   tablespoon sherry
1   tablespoon warm water
1   bunch celery

Dressing:
1   teaspoon soy sauce
½   teaspoon salt
1   tablespoon granulated sugar
1   tablespoon white vinegar
2   teaspoons sesame oil

Drain shrimp and place in small bowl. Add sherry and water and marinate for 30 minutes. Meanwhile, cut celery stalks in half lengthwise and then into 1 inch pieces, crosswise. Place in medium salad bowl. Drain shrimp and add to celery bowl (save marinade). In the small bowl, combine soy sauce, salt, sugar, vinegar, oil, and saved marinade and stir until sugar dissolves. Pour dressing mixture over shrimp and celery and toss well. Cover with plastic wrap and chill at least 1 hour. Makes 4 servings.

Doris

Doris Oliver

This is a pretty side dish that even youngsters seem to like.

Jean Sullivan, towels, 28" X 19", woven in black and white cotton using color and weave techniques, 1992.

TORTELLINI SALAD

1   pound tortellini pasta
Dressing:
2   cloves garlic
2   teaspoons Dijon mustard
¼   cup olive oil
¼   cup red wine vinegar
1   teaspoon dried oregano
½   teaspoon salt
Salad:
1   bunch green onions, sliced
½   cup ripe olives, sliced
1   sweet red bell pepper, julienne cut
½   cup parsley, chopped
½   cup Parmesan cheese, grated
1/3 cup sunflower seeds, toasted
1   teaspoon dried basil, or
      2 tablespoons fresh basil
      lots of freshly ground black pepper

Place tortellini in large stock pot of boiling water. Cook until al dente, rinse under cold water and drain. Place in a large bowl. Place garlic, mustard, oil, vinegar, oregano, and salt into electric blender and mix well. Add to tortellini the green onion, olives, red bell pepper, parsley, Parmesan, sunflower seeds, basil and pepper. Pour dressing from blender over salad mixture and toss well. Chill several hours to blend flavors. Serve at room temperature. Makes 8 servings.

Jean Sullivan

A pretty looking salad which always gets recipe requests. Be forewarned!

I often grin when I remember receiving my first loom. I had had a brief encounter with a small 2-harness loom and I decided I wanted to learn how to weave. As a surprise, my son-in-law brought back from a visit to his home in Sweden a 30 inch, 4-harness loom. It was in a very large, flat box, and when I opened it, I couldn't even imagine what it was. We were left to put it together with Swedish instructions. Talk about trial and error. However, I've put several together since and never needed instructions.

MAGIC RECIPE

This is a recipe for setting dye which comes from the Amish country. We've had good success with it in setting dark intense colors.

Heat to 140° steaming,
   2 gallons water
   1 tsp. copper sulphate crystals
   1 cup white vinegar

Stir to dissolve, add dampened fabric, stir 30 minutes, rinse cool water.

Reprinted from the newsletter published by **In the Beginning** fabric store, Seattle, WA.

GARDEN PASTA SALAD

2	tablespoons Dijon mustard
½	cup red wine vinegar
1	tablespoon garlic, minced
1	teaspoon granulated sugar
1	cup olive oil
	salt and pepper to taste
1	pound Fusilli pasta
6	plum tomatoes, cut into pieces
1	yellow pepper, diced
½	cup golden raisins
½	cup walnuts, chopped
3/4	pound snow peas, blanched
½	pound green beans, blanched
6	green onions, sliced
1	medium zucchini, diced
3/4	cup black olives
3/4	cup fresh basil leaves or
	1 tablespoon dried leaves
½	cup Parmesan cheese
2	cups ham, diced

In a small mixing bowl, blend the mustard, vinegar, garlic, sugar, olive oil, salt and pepper. Set dressing aside for at least an hour to let flavors blend. Cook pasta in boiling water until just tender (about 8 minutes); drain and rinse with cold water. In a large bowl, combine the pasta and one cup of the dressing. Add tomatoes, pepper, raisins and walnuts. Set aside. Twenty minutes before serving, add peas, green beans, onions, zucchini, olives, basil, cheese, ham and remaining dressing; toss. Makes 6 servings.

Jean Owens

41

Clara Mitchell, afghan, 87" X 30", green and white mohair and wools, woven in twill for the Seattle Weavers' Guild booth at A.N.W.G. Conference, Boise, 1989.

BROCCOLI SALAD

1 pound fresh, young, raw broccoli, cut
    into flowerettes
1 cup salted cashew nuts
2 tomatoes, cut into small chunks
1 small bunch green onions, chopped
1 bottle Kraft Creamy Cucumber dressing, or as desired

Add broccoli, cashew nuts, tomatoes, green onions and dressing in salad bowl. Chill. This salad can marinate a long while so is a handy salad to take to weavers' guild meetings or any pot lucks. It is a very decorative salad with the greens and red, and has a fresh crunch to it. Makes 6-8 servings.

Clara

Clara Mitchell

43

FRENCH POTATO SALAD

1   pound whole new red potatoes
¼   cup parsley, chopped
4   green onions, chopped
4   tablespoons olive oil
1   tablespoon fresh lemon juice,
¼   teaspoon salt

Boil potatoes, or cook in microwave oven until tender. Slice while still hot. Put in a bowl with parsley and onion. In a small bowl, whisk together the olive oil, lemon juice and salt. Pour dressing over warm potatoes. Add more lemon juice to taste. Serve warm. Makes 4 servings.

Jean Sullivan

Quick and easy and best when there are potatoes ready to be dug in the garden. It is more delicious than any potato salad with heavy dressing. The preparation is simple now that we have microwaves.

SAUERKRAUT SALAD

1   #2½ can sauerkraut, drained
1   large onion, chopped
1   cup celery, chopped
1   green bell pepper, chopped
1   small jar pimentos, chopped

Dressing:
1   cup granulated sugar
¼   cup oil
½   cup vinegar

In a large bowl, add sauerkraut, onion, celery, bell pepper and pimentos. In small bowl, mix the sugar, oil and vinegar, then pour over kraut mixture and mix well. Cover bowl with plastic wrap and refrigerate overnight or longer.

In memory of
Nellie Johnston

A benefit of Guild membership is the SAMPLE PAGES included in the newsletter, published since 1957. These samples usually contain fabric swatches, draw-downs, instructions and advice. This recipe was published in January 1970.

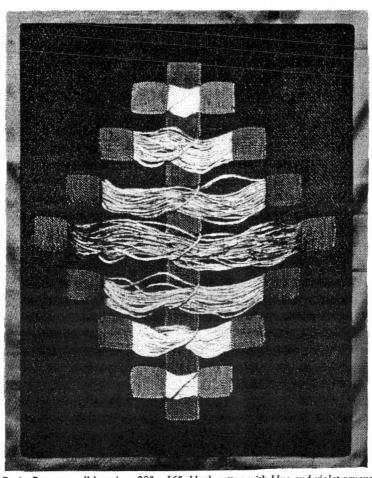

Becky Barnes, wall hanging, 20" x 16", black cotton with blue and violet rayons woven in variation of honeycomb technique, framed, 1992.

OUR FAVORITE BROCCOLI SALAD

3   cups raw broccoli flowerettes and
        tender stems (3 large stalks)
4   green onions, thinly sliced
4   slices bacon, cooked and crumbled
½   cup raisins
3/4 cup sunflower seeds
3/4 cup almonds, sliced
1   cup mayonnaise
¼   cup granulated sugar
3   tablespoons vinegar

In a large bowl, combine broccoli, onions, bacon, raisins, sunflower seeds and almonds. In small bowl, stir together mayonnaise, sugar and vinegar until well blended. Toss with salad ingredients. Serve immediately. Makes four 1 cup servings.

Becky

Becky Barnes

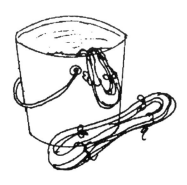

dye bucket & skein

INVESTMENT SALAD

1   10 ounce package frozen peas, thawed
1   can water chestnuts, chopped
½   can smoked almonds, chopped
¼   cup celery, chopped (more if desired)
¼   cup each mayonnaise and plain yoghurt, blended

In a medium bowl, mix peas, chestnuts, almonds, celery, mayonnaise
and yoghurt together and chill. Makes 6 servings.

Margaret

Margaret Schindler

*I double this easy recipe for pot lucks and usually bring home an
empty dish.*

dyebath container & jars

WILD RICE SALAD

12 cups boiling water
3   teaspoons salt
3   cups wild rice
1   cup carrots, diced
1   cup sweet red and/or yellow bell peppers, diced
1   cup mushrooms, sliced
1   cup small snow peas
½   cup pine nuts
2   tablespoons fresh parsley, chopped
Marinade:
1/3 cup olive oil
¼   cup lemon or lime juice
3   cloves garlic, pressed
1   teaspoon tarragon
1   teaspoon marjoram
    salt to taste

In salted boiling water, cook wild rice for 40 minutes; drain. Place the rice in a large bowl. Steam carrots, bell peppers, mushrooms, and snow peas separately until tender, though firm. Add the vegetables, pine nuts, and parsley to the rice. In a separate bowl, combine oil, lemon juice, garlic, tarragon, marjoram and salt; whisk together. Add the marinade to the rice mixture and stir. Refrigerate for several hours or overnight. Stir occasionally to make sure the marinade covers and flavors the rice and vegetables. Flavors increase with age. Makes 6 servings.

Bonnie

Bonnie Tarses

Besides flavor, I really appreciate color in my food - and in my weaving too. Here is a colorful, flavorful salad that I love to take to food celebrations.

Helen Sandvig, church paraments: stole and altar cloths, wools, woven in undulating twills in shades of green, mint and aqua, 1992.

CHUNKY BLUE CHEESE DRESSING

4 ounces Blue cheese, crumbled
3/4 cup salad oil
¼ cup apple cider vinegar
1 clove garlic, crushed
½ teaspoon salt
black pepper to taste
1 teaspoon oregano or marjoram
2 cups light sour cream

Optional:
a shake or two of Johnny's "Salad
Elegance" spice mixture
fresh parsley, chopped
herb vinegar (for a more tart taste)

Break up Blue cheese in a mixing bowl. Add oil and vinegar; mix gently with a beater. Add garlic, salt, pepper and oregano and mix. Add sour cream, slowly beat and then whip briefly. Store covered in refrigerator. Makes 2 pints.

Helen

Helen Sandvig

One year we had an emergency with Grandpa in the hospital and my son's birthday slipped up on me. When I apologized for not having a gift, he said, "Don't bother! I'll settle for a monthly batch of your Blue cheese dressing."

RANCH DRESSING SEASONING MIX

1 tablespoon black pepper
1 tablespoon garlic powder
2 tablespoons salt
4 tablespoons onion powder
  dried parsley as desired

In a small jar, combine pepper, garlic powder, salt, onion powder and parsley. Place lid on jar, shake and store for future use.

RANCH SALAD DRESSING

1 tablespoon Ranch Dressing Seasoning Mix
1 cup mayonnaise
1 cup buttermilk

In a covered container, combine season mix, mayonnaise, and buttermilk. Whisk until blended. Cover and refrigerate until used.

BLEU CHEESE SALAD DRESSING

1 tablespoon Ranch Dressing Seasoning Mix
1 cup mayonnaise
1 cup buttermilk
1 package Bleu cheese, crumbled

In a covered container, combine seasoning mix, mayonnaise, buttermilk and Bleu cheese. Whisk until blended. Cover and refrigerate until used.

Myra

Myra Reinelt

RASPBERRY MOLD

1 6 ounce package raspberry Jello
1 cup boiling water
1 6 ounce can frozen orange juice, undiluted
1 10 ounce pack frozen raspberries
1 20 ounce can crushed pineapple with juice

Topping (if desired):
1 3 ounce package cream cheese
1 tablespoon mayonnaise

In large bowl, dissolve Jello in boiling water; add orange juice, raspberries and pineapple. Pour into large mold and refrigerate until set. Mix the cheese and mayonnaise in a small bowl and spread on top of the Jello. Refrigerate until serving time.

Sally

Sally Still

Quick to fix plus a colorful and tasty addition to any meal.

RASPBERRY JELLO MOLD

Small recipe:
1 3 ounce package raspberry Jello
1 cup boiling water
1 cup raspberries, fresh or thawed, including juice
1 cup applesauce

Large recipe:
2 6 ounce packages raspberry Jello
4 cups boiling water
4 cups raspberries, fresh or thawed, including juice
4 cups applesauce

In bowl, dissolve Jello in boiling water, then add berries and applesauce and place in refrigerator until set. This will serve either as salad or dessert. Small recipe makes four 1 cup servings; large recipe makes twelve 1 cup servings.

Becky

Becky Barnes

This salad or desert has been traditional at final board meetings of the Seattle Weavers' Guild for the past 10 years.

FRUIT SALAD TOPPING

½ cup granulated sugar
3 tablespoons all-purpose flour
1 whole egg, slightly beaten
½ cup pineapple juice
½ cup apricot juice
2 tablespoons butter
1 cup whipping cream, whipped

Combine sugar and flour in a medium sauce pan, then blend in egg. Gradually stir in juices. Cook over low heat until thickened, stirring constantly. Remove from heat and stir in butter; cool. Fold in whipped whipping cream. Dollop salad topping onto individual servings of fresh fruit.

Kay

Kay Schrader

Breads

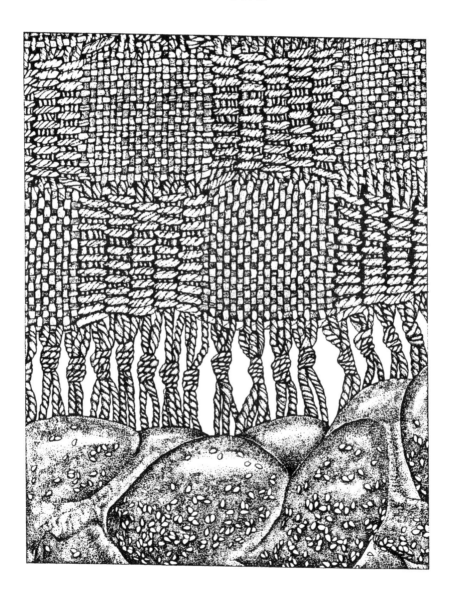

QUICK BUTTER CROISSANTS

½	pound butter, firm
6	cups unsifted all-purpose flour
2	packages yeast
1	cup warm water
1	small can evaporated milk
1½	teaspoon salt
1/3	cup granulated sugar
2	whole eggs, beaten
¼	cup cooking oil or butter, melted, cooled

Preheat oven to 325°F. In a large bowl, cut butter into 5 cups flour. Chunks should be about the size of dried kidney beans. If too finely cut, croissants will not be as flaky. In mixing bowl, soften yeast in warm water; add evaporated milk, 1 cup flour, salt, sugar, eggs and cooking oil (or cooled melted butter). Beat. Pour the yeast mixture over the flour-butter mixture. Mix with a spatula only until the flour is moistened. Cover (or place in plastic bag) and refrigerate from 4 hours to 4 days. Remove from refrigerator, knead 5-6 times (you may wish to let it sit at room temperature for about 15 minutes). Divide dough into 4 parts. Roll each on a floured board to form large circle. Cut into 6 or more equal parts (wedges, like a pie). Starting at the wide end roll up; place on flat cookie sheet, bending to form crescent shape. Allow to rise until almost doubled (2-4 hours). Bake croissants for 35 minutes. Baked rolls may be placed in freezer to be used when needed. Allow to thaw slightly and reheat at 325°F for a few minutes. Do not reheat in microwave or they will toughen.

Melba

Melba Short

Fresh breads always make a hit when you want to contribute to a dinner party. This is a great do-ahead recipe too.

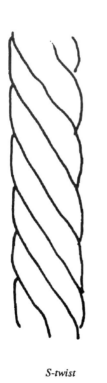

S-twist   Z-twist

PESTO BREAD

4-5   tablespoons pesto sauce
6-8   ounces mayonnaise
1   can black olives, sliced
1   cup green onions, diced
1   large tomato, diced or one red bell
         pepper, diced
1½   cups fresh Parmesan cheese, grated
         dash cayenne pepper
         French bread slices or small rye bread

Preheat oven to 350°F. In medium bowl, mix together pesto sauce, mayonnaise, olives, onions, cheese and cayenne and spread on French or rye bread slices. Bake until cheese is melted and golden brown, about 5 minutes.

Linda

Linda Jaeger

spinning wheel

FLAT BRÖD

1	cup Bran Buds (or All Bran) cereal
1	cup quick oats
1	teaspoon salt
2	cups buttermilk
¼	cup sugar
½	cup margarine
1	cup all-purpose flour
1½	teaspoon baking soda
1½	teaspoon baking powder

Preheat oven to 325°F. In a medium bowl, soak the bran and oats
with the salt and buttermilk for 10 minutes. Add the sugar and
margarine and stir. Sift together the flour, soda and baking powder
and add to the previous ingredients. Mix and add additional flour to
make a stiff dough. Chill for 1-2 hours. Roll out on floured area to
1/8 inch thickness. Cut into cracker size pieces. Bake on cookie
sheets for 12-15 minutes or until light brown. Cool. Store in air tight
container. (I use part rye or whole wheat *with* white flour to roll out
dough.) Makes 12 dozen small crackers.

Helen

Helen Sandvig

*Seaview Guild's May salad luncheon wouldn't be the same without
Olivia Cole's Flat Bröd. They are tasty, tender crackers you can't
stop eating!*

61

Bonnie Tarses, shawl, 101" X 29", silk ikat woven in black, wine and white space-dyed fibers using "easy-ikat" technique, 1992.

MANDEL BRODT (ALMOND BREAD)

3   whole eggs
½   cup canola oil
½   cup granulated sugar
1   teaspoon vanilla extract
3   cups all-purpose flour
1   teaspoon baking powder
1   cup golden raisins (optional)
1   cup almonds, slivered
    cinnamon and sugar for sprinkling slices

Preheat oven to 350°F. Combine eggs, oil, sugar and vanilla in medium mixing bowl and beat well to blend. Sift flour and baking powder together and blend in. Add raisins and almonds. Mix all together until smooth and easy to handle. Shape into four elongated loaves and place on greased and floured cookie sheet. Bake for 30 minutes or until loaves start to turn brown. Remove from oven, let cool slightly, and while still warm, cut in ½ inch diagonal slices. (The bread will crumble if cut immediately.) Place slices on their sides on cookie sheet, sprinkle with cinnamon and sugar and return to oven for about 5 minutes. Makes about 40 slices.

Bonnie

Bonnie Tarses

When I was in high school in the 1950s, my mother got a cookbook put out by the Hadassah in Baltimore. She systematically tried all the recipes and then gave me my own copy when I went off to college. Now my cookbook is in shreds, but this recipe remains my favorite. It is great for dunking and is delicious without being too sweet.

PUMPKIN BREAD

3½	cups all-purpose flour
3	cups granulated sugar
½	teaspoon baking powder
2	teaspoons baking soda
1	teaspoons salt
1	teaspoon ground nutmeg
1	teaspoon ground cinnamon
1	teaspoon ground cloves
4	whole eggs
1	cup vegetable oil
2	cups solid pack pureed pumpkin
1	cup chopped walnuts or pecans

Preheat oven to 350°F. Combine dry ingredients in large bowl. Combine eggs, oil and pumpkin in medium bowl and stir till well blended. Add to dry ingredients. Fold in walnuts. Mixture will be thick. Spoon into 2 greased and floured 9 X 5 X 3 inch loaf pans (or four mini-loaves), filling pans three-quarters full. Bake for 1 hour, 5 minutes (40-45 minutes for mini loaves) or until toothpick inserted in loaf comes out clean. Let cool 10-15 minutes in pan, then place on rack to cool completely. Makes 2 large (or 4 small) loaves. This recipe can be varied by using part brown sugar and part whole wheat flour.

Martha

Martha Cram

Margie Albrecht is one of my favorite friends who loves to play outdoors, and she is a very good cook. Her bread is delicious with slices of cheese and apples. It also freezes well.

HEALTHFUL DATE BREAD

1	8 ounce package pitted whole dates, snipped
1	cup raisins
1½	cups water, boiling
1	cup whole wheat flour
1	cup all-purpose flour
1	teaspoon baking soda
1	teaspoon baking powder
¼	teaspoon salt
2	egg whites, slightly beaten
1	teaspoon vanilla
½	cup chopped almonds

Preheat oven to 350°F. In medium bowl, combine dates and raisins. Pour boiling water over all and set aside to cook slightly. Let cool. In large bowl, stir together flour, baking soda, baking powder and salt. Stir egg whites and vanilla into cooked date mixture. Add date mixture and almonds to flour mixture and stir until well blended. Mixture will be thick.

Spread evenly in a 9 X 5 X 3 inch loaf pan. Bake for 40-50 minutes or until a toothpick inserted in loaf comes out clean. Cool in pan 10 minutes. Remove from pan and cool thoroughly on a wire rack. Wrap and store overnight before serving. Slice thinly. Makes 1 large loaf.

Margaret

Margaret Schindler

If you are watching sugar and cholesterol intake, this is a delicious way to get something sweet.

Cyndi White, "Embellished Bomber Jacket," white and mauve "boiled" wool, woven in sections, embroidered designs with clay beads, 1988.

MONKEY BREAD

1   cup milk, scalded, cooled
¼   cup warm water
1   package yeast, dissolved
3/4 cup butter, melted
3   whole eggs, well-beaten
½   cup sugar
4   cups all-purpose flour
1   cup butter, melted
Optional:
½   cup nuts, chopped
½   cup candied cherries

Preheat oven to 400°F. Beat milk, yeast, butter, eggs and sugar together in large mixing bowl with electric mixer on medium speed. Blend in flour, 1 cupful at a time. Mix well, then set to rise in draft-free area with clean towel over bowl for ½-1 hour, until double in size. Punch down and roll out on floured board to about 1 inch thick. Cut out circles of dough with round cookie cutter. Dip cut dough in melted butter, covering both sides. Arrange in angel food or high-sided ring mold pan, 9-12 inches wide, in over-lapping layers, 2 deep. The mold should be about half full. (Optional: Sprinkle nuts and cherries between layers.) Cover again and let rise another ½-1 hour. Bake in center of oven for 20 minutes or until golden brown. It will puff up over edge of pan. Invert onto plate, serve warm for dinner or breakfast. Guests peel off layers. You don't need to butter this bread! Makes 10-12 servings.

Cyndi

Cyndi White

I love fresh baked bread, and this one is without the mess. You may have butter all over you after you make Monkey Bread but no sticky hands. I can smell the aroma just thinking about it.

BANANA NUT BREAD

3/4 cup granulated sugar
½   cup margarine
2   whole eggs
1   cup all-purpose flour
1   cup graham flour
1   teaspoon baking soda
½   teaspoon salt
1   cup chopped nuts of your choice
1   cup mashed bananas
1   tablespoon lemon juice

Preheat oven to 350°F. In large bowl, cream sugar and margarine together. Add eggs and beat well. In a separate bowl, mix the flours, baking soda, salt and nuts together. In another bowl, combine bananas and lemon juice. Add alternately with flour mixture to creamed mixture. Stir only until flour is moistened. Grease a 9 X 5 inch loaf pan. Pour the batter into the pan and spread evenly. Bake for one hour. Test. Cool 10 minutes on a wire rack before removing bread from pan, then let sit until completely cool. Makes 1 loaf.

Jennie

Jennie Jeffries

Adapted from the High Fiber Cookbook, by M. Cavaiani

hand spindle

CHEESE BRAID ROLLS

1	package active dry yeast
¼	cup warm water (105-115°F)
¼	cup butter or margarine, melted
½	cup milk
1	whole egg
1	tablespoon granulated sugar
½	teaspoon salt
2-2½	cups all-purpose flour
½	cup sharp Cheddar cheese, grated
1	egg white, slightly beaten

Preheat oven to 375°F. In a large bowl, dissolve yeast in the warm water and let stand 5 minutes. Melt the butter in a small sauce pan, warm the milk and add butter, egg, sugar and salt to the yeast mixture. Slowly, add the flour ½ cup at a time, stirring between additions. Stir until stiff. Knead on a floured board until smooth. Place in a greased bowl and cover to rise. In about ½ hour, knead in the grated cheese and shape rolls in a 2-strand braid or twist: cut the dough into 16 pieces and divide each piece into 2 six inch ropes; cross the two ropes, then fold opposite ends, crossing them over each other, alternately (see diagram). Place on a greased cookie sheet. Let rise for 30 minutes. Brush with beaten egg white. Bake for 15 minutes or until golden brown. Makes 16 rolls.

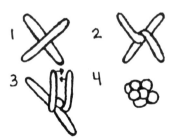

Bonnie

Bonnie Nelson

Molly Gerhard, fur pillow, handspun wool woven in shades of brown; two skeins of cream and golden handspun wool, 1989.

SWG SWEET SOURDOUGH STARTER

If you are not a lucky owner of the Seattle Weavers' Guild Sweet Sourdough Starter, by asking Lois Gaylord or Molly Gerhard, you're sure to find someone has a steady supply and will be happy to share. For those who already have a supply growing in their kitchen, the following recipes have been found to be delicious...

Upon receiving your portion, place it in a glass or plastic bowl, covered. Do not refrigerate.

Day 1: The day you receive your starter, do nothing.
Days 2, 3, and 4: Stir with a wooden spoon.
Day 5: Add 1 cup each of all-purpose flour, granulated sugar and milk. Stir.
Days 6, 7, 8, and 9: Stir with a wooden spoon.
Day 10: Add 1 cup each of all-purpose flour, granulated sugar and milk. Stir. Keep 2 cups of the mixture - 1 for your starter and 1 for the recipe. Can be maintained in the refrigerator. Give the rest as 1-cup starters to friends with these same instructions.

Seattle Weavers' Guild

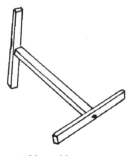

niddy-noddy

71

AMISH FRIENDSHIP BREAD

1	cup SWG Sweet Sourdough Starter
2/3	cup oil
2	cups all-purpose flour
1	cup granulated sugar
1¼	teaspoon baking powder
½	teaspoon baking soda
½	teaspoon salt
1	teaspoon cinnamon
1	teaspoon vanilla
3	whole eggs
1	cup candied fruit, nuts, raisins or whatever you like

Preheat oven to 350°F. In a large bowl, add sourdough starter, oil, flour, sugar, baking powder, baking soda, salt, cinnamon, vanilla, eggs and fruits or nuts; stir well. Pour into 2 well greased and sugared (not floured) loaf pans. Bake 40-50 minutes. Cool 10 minutes before removing from pans. Bundt pans can also be used.

NOTE: Lois Gaylord puts her starter in the refrigerator when she won't be using it for awhile. She also cuts the amount of sugar in half, as she feels it is too sweet.

Molly

Molly Gerhard

When you run out of people to give your sourdough starter to, try this recipe to use up the excess. These loaves make welcome gifts also!

FRIENDSHIP MUFFINS

Basic Batter:

2   cups SWG sweet sourdough starter
3/4   cup oil
1   cup granulated sugar
3   whole eggs, beaten
2   teaspoon vanilla
2   cups all-purpose flour
1½ teaspoons cinnamon
1   teaspoon salt
1½ teaspoons baking soda

Preheat oven to 350°F. In a large bowl, add starter, oil, sugar, eggs, vanilla, flour, cinnamon, salt and soda and stir until blended. Pour into greased or lined muffin tins and bake for 20-25 minutes. You can bake in larger muffin tins, loaf pans, or bundt pans. The baking time can go up to 45 minutes, depending on the size of pan.

Variations:
for orange flavor, add to basic batter:
     peel of 1 orange, grated
½ teaspoon ground cloves
½ teaspoon nutmeg
Substitute for one cup of all-purpose flour:
½ cup oatmeal
½ cup whole wheat flour
Brush cooked muffins with freshly squeezed orange juice and sprinkle with granulated sugar. Leave muffins in pan for 5 minutes.

for cranberry-walnut flavor, add to basic batter:
1   cup cranberries
1   cup apples, grated or finely chopped
1   cup walnuts, chopped
3/4 teaspoon cinnamon
3/4 teaspoon allspice
1½ teaspoon grated orange peel

FRIENDSHIP MUFFINS, cont'd.

for banana-chocolate chip flavor:
Substitute for 1 cup all-purpose flour:
1   cup whole wheat flour
Add to basic batter:
1   cup bananas, mashed
1   cup nuts, chopped
1   cup chocolate chips

for applesauce-date-nut flavor:
Add to basic batter:
1   cup applesauce
1   cup dates, chopped
1   cup nuts, chopped
3/4 teaspoon cinnamon
3/4 teaspoon allspice
Substitute brown sugar for 1 cup granulated sugar

for applesauce-oatmeal flavor:
Substitute for 1 cup of all-purpose flour:
1   cup oatmeal
1   cup applesauce
1   cup nuts, chopped
½   teaspoon cloves
1   cup currants or raisins
1   teaspoon cinnamon

Molly Gerhard

During the Handweavers' Guild of America Conference (1982) in Seattle, my college friend, Kathy Murphy, asked if she and some fellow weavers could stay with me. She contributed the muffin recipe. I was a spinner and knitter then but as I took Kathy and her friends to the exhibits around town I became intrigued with handwoven garments. Before she returned to California, Kathy treated me to my first warp and showed me how to warp a rigid heddle loom. That was the start of my weaving addiction.

74

SOURDOUGH CINNAMON ROLLS

½   cup warm water
¼-½   teaspoon sugar
2   teaspoons active dry yeast
2   cups SWG Sweet Sourdough Starter
¼   cup oil
1½   teaspoon salt
2   cups whole wheat flour
½-1   cups all-purpose flour
1-2   tablespoons butter or margarine, melted
        cinnamon
        brown sugar
        raisins

Preheat oven to 350°F. In large bowl, mix yeast and sugar in water, allowing it to form bubbles or become foamy. Mix starter, oil, and salt into yeast mixture. Gradually add flour with spoon until dough comes easily away from bowl. Turn onto floured board and knead for 5 minutes adding flour as necessary. Dough should be smooth and elastic though it may be a little softer than regular bread dough. Let dough rest for 5-10 minutes. Roll out into a rectangle ¼-½ inch thick. Brush with melted butter; sprinkle with cinnamon, brown sugar and raisins. Roll up jelly-roll fashion along the long edge and seal edge with a little water. Slice across roll 1-1½ inches wide. Place in greased pans about ½ inch apart flat side down. Let rise, covered with a cloth for about 45 minutes or until approximately double in size. Bake for 20 minutes. (You can also place slices in pan the night before and let rise in the refrigerator and bake in the morning.) Note: If using an unsweetened sourdough starter, add 2 tablespoons honey or ¼ cup granulated sugar to dough.

Lois

Lois Gaylord

75

Lois Gaylord, "Scheherezade," origami fabric box, 4" X 4", cotton, embellished with beads, machine stitching and fabric paint, 1991.

SIX WEEK MUFFINS

6 cups bran
2 cups boiling water
1 cup shortening
2 cups granulated sugar
4 whole eggs, beaten
1 quart buttermilk
5 cups all-purpose flour
5 teaspoons baking soda
2 teaspoons salt

Preheat oven to 400°F. In a small bowl, pour boiling water over 2 cups bran and let stand. Mix in shortening. In a medium bowl, mix 4 cups bran with granulated sugar, eggs and buttermilk. Sift all-purpose flour with baking soda and salt. Into milk mixture add soaked bran mixture and dry ingredients. Grease muffin pans and bake for 20 minutes. You may add dates, nuts, chopped apple or whatever. Will keep in refrigerator for 6 weeks. Makes 15 muffins.

Barbara

Barbara Mahan

ALWAYS BE PREPARED! Offer muffins and coffee at the drop of a shuttle.

77

GAIL'S BRAN MUFFINS

1½   cups bran cereal
1   cup all-purpose flour
1   teaspoon baking soda
1   teaspoon baking powder
3/4   cup milk, whole or 2%
½   tablespoon cooking oil
2   whole eggs, beaten
½   cup honey or ¼ cup molasses and
       ¼ cup honey

Preheat oven to 400°F. Grease 12 muffin tins, or use paper liners.
In medium bowl, stir the cereal, flour, soda, and baking powder.
Blend milk, oil, eggs and honey in a separate bowl. Combine liquid
with dry ingredients until just moistened. Fill muffin cups 2/3 full.
Bake for 15 minutes. Makes 1 dozen.

Marcy

Marcy Johnson

These are great because they are not too sweet.

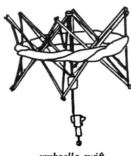

umbrella swift

POPEYE CEREAL MUFFINS

2½   cups Stone-Buhr cereal mix (or 7 grain)
2½   cups milk
½   cup raisins
2/3   cup shortening, softened
1   whole egg
2   cups Stone-Buhr all-purpose flour, sifted
2/3   cup granulated sugar
4   teaspoons baking powder
1   teaspoon salt

Preheat oven to 400°F. Combine cereal and milk in medium bowl; let stand 10 minutes. Add raisins, shortening and egg to mixture. Beat well with fork. Sift together flour, sugar, baking powder and salt. Add to cereal mixture; stir only until combined. Fill greased muffin pans 3/4 full. Bake 25-30 minutes or until lightly browned. Serve hot. Makes 12 medium muffins.

MARIANNE

Marianne Costello

Roberta Lowes, "Collage Coat," handpainted, woven fabrics of rayon and silk with additions of ultra suede and cotton in shades of greens, browns and purples, handmade fused glass buttons, 1991.

ROBERTA'S FRUIT MUFFINS

1 cup all-purpose flour
1 cup whole wheat flour
1 teaspoon baking powder
1 teaspoon baking soda
¼ teaspoon salt
½ teaspoon ground cinnamon
½ cup chopped nuts
½ cup dried fruits, chopped, your choice
1 cup granulated sugar
½ cup vegetable oil
2 whole eggs, lightly beaten
1 cup crushed pineapple, drained
1 small banana, mashed
Streusel topping:
½ cup granulated sugar
1/3 cup all-purpose flour
4 teaspoons butter or margarine, chilled

Preheat oven to 350°F. Sift together the flours, baking powder, soda, salt and cinnamon and place in large bowl. Add nuts and your choice of fruit. In separate bowl, mix the sugar, oil, eggs, banana and pineapple; add to dry ingredients. Mix thoroughly. Grease 14-16 muffin cups or use paper liners; fill 2/3 full. Mix remaining sugar and flour together; cut in butter until crumbly and well blended. Top each muffin with 1 tablespoon topping. Bake 20 minutes or until toothpick comes out clean when tested. Makes 14-16 muffins.

Roberta

Roberta Lowes

These muffins are a favorite Sunday morning substitute for our regular healthy cereal. I often make them without the streusel topping.

BLUEBERRY MUFFINS

2   cups all-purpose flour, sifted
½   cup granulated sugar
2   teaspoons baking powder
½   teaspoon baking soda
½   cup butter or margarine
2   whole eggs, slightly beaten
½   cup buttermilk (2-3 more tablespoons
      may be necessary)
1   cup fresh or frozen blueberries
½   teaspoon lemon or orange peel, grated

Preheat oven to 375°F. Sift dry ingredients together. Cut in the butter or margarine until the size of small peas. Beat the eggs slightly and add the buttermilk. Combine the dry ingredients to the liquid all at once. You may need to add 2-3 more tablespoons of buttermilk to make a soft dough. Gently stir in the blueberries and orange peel. Bake in greased muffin tins for 25-30 minutes or until lightly browned. Make 12 large muffins. These freeze well.

Marguerite

Marguerite Oprea

We planted seven blueberry bushes thirty-four years ago and they now supply more berries than we can use each year. Of all the blueberry recipes I've collected, this is our favorite.

MORNING GLORY MUFFINS

2	cups carrots, grated
½	cup apple, peeled and chopped
½	cup golden raisins, soaked in hot water
½	cup walnuts, chopped
½	cup coconut, flaked
1	cup granulated sugar
¼	cup brown sugar, packed
½	cup margarine, softened
3	whole eggs
2	teaspoons vanilla
1½	cups all-purpose flour
½	cup All-Bran cereal
2	teaspoons baking powder
1	teaspoon cinnamon
½	teaspoon salt
1	teaspoon nutmeg

Preheat oven to 350°F. In a bowl, combine carrots, apple, drained raisins, walnuts and coconut and toss. In another bowl, beat together sugars, margarine, eggs and vanilla with mixer. In a third bowl, combine flour, All-Bran, baking powder, cinnamon, salt and nutmeg. Add carrot mixture to third bowl and mix well, then add sugar mixture and mix just to moisten flour. Spoon batter into 12 greased muffin cups and bake for 25-30 minutes or until done.

The Unknown Weaver

Every weaver knows about gremlins. They snarl your warp, make knots, mix up the threading and misplace balls of yarn. The gremlins submitted this recipe without name or signature. So make a batch of these muffins - even a double recipe doesn't last long - and eventually all will come right. This recipe, with a few minor changes and additions, came from the Seattle Post Intelligencer, date unknown.

PANNUKAKKO (FINNISH "PAN" CAKE)

4   whole eggs
3   cups milk
1¼   cups flour
½   teaspoon salt
4   ounces margarine
     sugar for topping

Preheat oven to 450°F. In large bowl, beat the eggs and add about ½ cup milk. Gradually add the remaining milk, flour and salt. Beat hard with a spoon or electric mixer until smooth and thickened. Melt the margarine in the microwave or on stove top. Pour melted margarine into a 15 X 10 X 1 inch jelly roll pan, distributing evenly. Pour batter over margarine. Bake for 25-30 minutes or until golden brown and puffy. Sprinkle sugar on top and serve immediately on warm plates. A festive holiday breakfast or brunch. Makes 4 servings.

Cynthia W. Johnson

ball by winder, cone,
ball by hand, and skein

COTTAGE CHEESE PANCAKES

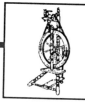

3 large whole eggs, slightly beaten
1 tablespoon cooking oil
1 cup cream style cottage cheese,
  small curd
½ teaspoon baking powder
¼ cup all-purpose flour

Mix ingredients together until just blended. Lightly coat griddle with margarine or cooking oil and preheat on medium heat. (The batter will stick if the pan is too hot.) Cook pancakes, flipping when brown on first side, about 3 minutes. Serve with sour cream and jam or fresh fruit. Makes about ten 4 inch pancakes.

Jane

Jane Andrews

This recipe came from a house guest many years ago and has become a family favorite for weekend breakfast or brunch.

COTTAGE CHEESE PANCAKES

2   whole eggs
1/3 cup all-purpose flour
1   cup large curd cottage cheese
1   teaspoon sugar

Separate egg yolks from whites. Beat egg whites until stiff. Beat yolks in a separate bowl; add cottage cheese, flour and sugar; stir till mixed. Fold in beaten egg whites. The cottage cheese varies in creaminess and you may need to add a bit more flour if the pancakes do not hold together when turned. Brush a non-stick griddle or pan with a film of oil. Make 3 inch pancakes. Turn when top of pancake bubbles. Serve with fresh fruit jam or fresh berries. Makes 2 servings.

Marguerite

Marguerite Oprea

So easy and nutritious, these little pancakes are on our breakfast menu almost once a week.

The Main Course

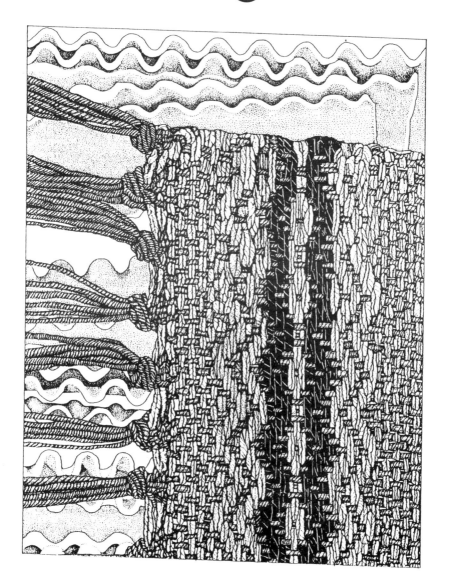

CIOPPINI

¼ cup green pepper, chopped
2 tablespoons onion, minced
1 clove garlic, minced
1 tablespoon olive oil
1 16 ounce can tomatoes, cut up
½ cup red wine
3 tablespoons parsley, minced
½ teaspoon salt
¼ teaspoon oregano
¼ teaspoon basil
   pepper to taste
½ pound cod, cut in pieces
½ pound prawns
1 can clams, not drained

In large soup kettle, cook green pepper, onion and garlic in oil until tender. Add tomatoes, red wine, parsley, salt, oregano, basil and pepper. Bring to a boil, reduce heat and simmer 20 minutes. Add cod and prawns and simmer 5 minutes. Add clams and simmer 5 minutes more. Serve with French bread and salad. (You can vary the seafood in this with whatever you like that is fresh.)

Joanne

Joanne McConnell

warping board

ALMOND FISH

1/3 cup butter
½ cup almonds, sliced
1 tablespoon lemon peel
1 teaspoon dill weed
1 pound white fish fillets (halibut, cod, pollock)

Preheat oven to 350°F. In the oven, melt butter in baking dish large enough to hold the fish. Add almonds; stir and toast (about 10 minutes). Stir in peel and dill weed. Dip fish fillets into butter mixture and coat evenly. Spoon remaining mixture over fish. Bake 15-25 minutes or until fish flakes with a fork.

Gwen Zierdt

I like the contrast of the crunchy almonds with the tender fish.

warping mill

Jean Wilson, "The Girls," 11½" X 11½", wools, tapestry woven in shades of greens, oranges and browns, from the book Weaving You Can Use*, 1975.*

For the guest teacher/lecturer, weavers usually have a pot luck buffet. Over the years, I have been treated to some mighty fine food. At one especially sumptuous, sophisticated feast, a husband looked it over and said, "Only weavers would bring quiche, home-baked herb bread, Caesar salad, paté, and brandied fruit." Plus other good dishes. Weavers are good cooks, too. We savor these curry flavored eggs for brunch, lunch or a light dinner.

CHEESE CURRY EGGS

4	hard boiled eggs
½	cup milk, hot
½	cup Cheddar cheese, diced
1	tablespoon all-purpose flour
1	tablespoon butter or margarine
¼	teaspoon paprika
½	teaspoon curry powder
½	teaspoon salt
	one or more slices of bread made into crumbs

Preheat oven to 400°F. Halve or slice the eggs. Place eggs in a buttered shallow baking dish. Put milk, cheese, flour, butter, paprika, curry and salt in a blender. Blend on high speed for about 10 seconds or until well mixed. Pour over the eggs. Top with bread crumbs. Dot with about 1 tablespoon of butter. (For evenly buttered crumbs, lightly butter the slices and crumble them in the blender.) Bake for 15 minutes, or until crumbs are brown. These eggs are delicious served with a thin slice of ham or turkey-ham.

A tasty variation: Use herb bread for the crumbs. Sour dough bread gives a subtle variation of flavor.

Jean

Jean Wilson

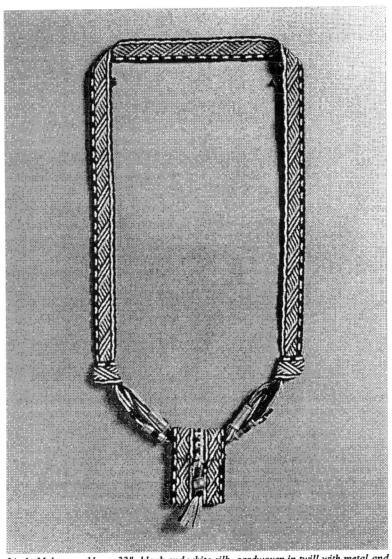

Linda Malan, necklace, 33", black and white silk, cardwoven in twill with metal and glass beads, 1990.

GARDEN PASTA

1   6 ounce jar marinated artichoke hearts,
      drained and cut into small pieces
2   tablespoons reserved artichoke marinade
1   medium onion, finely chopped
2   cloves garlic, minced
2   cups tomatoes, peeled and diced (or 1
      14½ ounce can ready-cut tomatoes,
      add juice with tomatoes to mixture)
1   small bay leaf
1   tablespoon fresh basil, finely chopped
      (or 1 teaspoon dried basil)
8   ounces linguini noodles
1/3 cup black olives, sliced
2   tablespoons pine nuts
3   tablespoons parsley, chopped
2   tablespoons olive oil
1/3 cup fresh Parmesan cheese, grated

In large non-stick skillet, pour 2 tablespoons of artichoke marinade and sauté onions. When onions are soft, add garlic and sauté a moment more. Add tomatoes, bay leaf and basil, cover and simmer 10 minutes. Uncover and continue simmering until sauce mixture thickens slightly, about 10 minutes. Add artichoke pieces, olives, pine nuts and parsley. Remove bay leaf. Meanwhile, cook the noodles in boiling water until tender. Drain; toss with olive oil and Parmesan. Top pasta with sauce and serve. (Sauce can be prepared in advance and then rewarmed to enhance flavor.) Makes 4 one cup servings.

Linda Malan

CJ'S LASAGNA

Meat sauce:
2   pounds ground beef
2-3 tablespoons olive oil
1   cup onion, chopped
2-3 cloves garlic, minced
1   tablespoon each dried basil and
        oregano (use more if fresh)
1   28 ounce can plum tomatoes and juice
2   6 ounce cans tomato paste
½   cup dry red wine
8   ounces lasagna noodles, dry uncooked
1   pound Mozzarella cheese, thinly sliced
Cheese layer:
2   cups part skim Ricotta cheese
½   cup Parmesan or Romano cheese, grated
1   tablespoon fresh parsley, chopped
        pinch black pepper
2   egg whites, beaten
1-2 tablespoons white Vermouth

Preheat oven to 350°F. Brown ground beef in olive oil until well
crumbled. Add onion and cook until transparent. Add garlic, herbs,
tomatoes and tomato paste. Stir well and let simmer for 30 minutes,
stirring occasionally to prevent sticking. Cool slightly. Cover bottom
of 9 X 13 inch shallow baking pan with ¼ cup meat sauce. Top with
½ uncooked lasagna noodles. Spread ½ cheese sauce and ½
Mozzarella over noodles. Cover with ½ remaining meat sauce,
lasagna noodles, cheese sauce, Mozzarella and finish with again with
meat sauce. Bake uncovered for 40 minutes. Let stand for 1 day
before serving. It freezes wonderfully - just thaw and reheat. Makes
12 servings.

Caroline
Caroline Jorstad

94

None of the Jorstads can claim actual Italian blood, but we are all Italian "wanna-be"s! On Mondays, noodles get made at my house. When we make lasagna noodles, I make two of these casseroles and freeze them. Almost all company to our home has eaten this.

threading hook

LASAGNA

1	10 ounce package chopped spinach
8-10	lasagna noodles
1	pound ground beef
½	cup onion, chopped
½	teaspoon garlic salt (to taste)
1	8 ounce can tomato sauce
1	6 ounce can tomato paste
1	cup water
1	2 ounce can mushrooms, save liquid
1	teaspoon garlic salt (to taste)
3/4	teaspoon oregano, crushed
3/4	teaspoon basil, crushed
½	teaspoon salt (to taste)
½	teaspoon sugar
	dash pepper
1/8	teaspoon crushed red pepper
1	whole egg
3/4	cup small curd cottage cheese
¼	cup Parmesan cheese, grated
1 1/3	cup Mozzarella cheese, shredded

Preheat oven to 350°F. Cook spinach according to package directions until thawed. Cook noodles according to directions; rinse and drain. In a large skillet, brown beef with onion and garlic salt (be careful with amounts of salts); drain fat; reduce heat and add sauce, paste and water; stir. Add mushrooms in their liquid. Stir in seasonings and simmer for 20 minutes. In a small bowl, combine spinach with egg and three cheeses (use 1/3 cup Mozzarella). Pour ½ meat sauce into a 9 X 13 inch pan. Cover with layer of noodles; spread spinach-cheese mixture over noodles. Top with layer of noodles and meat sauce. Sprinkle with remaining Mozzarella. Bake for 25-30 minutes; let stand 5-10 minutes before cutting. Makes 6-8 servings.

Kay

Kay Schrader

PESTO SAUCE WITH PASTA

½   cup pine nuts, hazelnuts or both
         combined
3-4   large garlic cloves
½   cup Parmesan cheese, grated
1/3   cup olive oil
1½-2 cups fresh basil leaves, packed
1   pound pasta, cooked

In food processor or blender, grind nuts with garlic. In bowl, combine Parmesan cheese and nut mixture. Pour oil into food processor (or blender), stuff basil on top of oil and blend until smooth. Pour into nut and cheese mixture and mix well. Toss with pasta. Makes 3 servings.

Kay.

Kay Schrader

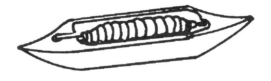

boat shuttle

97

*Gay Jensen, scarf, 82" X 7", black and white rayon/cotton, woven
in plain weave, handpainted design added after fabric was removed
from loom, 1992.*

*My Grandma Terracciano was less than 5 feet tall, gave birth to 11
(yes, eleven!) children at home, was illiterate, and was a fantastic
Italian cook. It is likely that this unusual dish was largely her own
creation or based on a dish she remembered from her childhood in
Italy. I have never seen anything like it in any cookbook. You don't
have to wait for Christmas to try it.*

Gay Jensen

GRANDMA TERRACCIANO'S
CHRISTMAS SPAGHETTI

1 cup olive oil
3 cloves garlic, smashed
1 cup pine nuts
1 cup walnut halves
1 8-10 ounce jar green olives with pits
    still in them, well drained
1 rounded tablespoon capers, drained
1 quart hot water
    salt and pepper to taste
1 pound vermicelli, spaghettini or
    spaghetti, uncooked

In a large, heavy saucepan, heat the olive oil over medium-low heat. Add the smashed garlic. Stir and cook the garlic until brown, then remove and discard the garlic with a slotted spoon (its only purpose was to flavor the oil). Add the pine nuts to the oil, cook and stir until nicely browned (don't let them burn), then remove with slotted spoon and save them to add later. Add the walnuts to the oil, cook and stir until nicely browned, then remove and save like the pine nuts. Add the olives to the oil (use a long handled spoon since the olives tend to splatter) and cook and stir until the skins look blistered and the olives begin to pucker. Remove the olives from the oil and save. Add capers, cook and stir until nicely browned (capers cook relatively quickly so watch carefully). Remove pan from heat; return the pine nuts, walnuts and olives to the pan with the capers and oil. Let cool a few minutes and then carefully add 1 quart hot water, salt and pepper as desired. Return to heat and simmer sauce uncovered for about 1 hour, stirring occasionally. Cook pasta according to package directions; drain. Add the sauce and toss. Let sit a bit so pasta absorbs the sauce.

Note: Don't have the oil too hot when you are browning the ingredients or they will burn before releasing their flavors into the oil.

GHIVETCH

1	cup carrots, thinly sliced (2 medium)
1	cup fresh green beans, sliced on diagonal
1	cup small red potatoes with skin, diced
½	cup celery, sliced (1 large stalk)
2	medium tomatoes, cored and quartered
1	small yellow squash, thinly sliced
½	small head cauliflower, broken into small flowerettes
¼-½	cup green pepper, cut into julienne strips
¼-½	cup red pepper, cut into julienne strips
½	cup frozen green peas
1	small zucchini, sliced
1	cup beef bouillon
1/3	cup olive oil
3-4	cloves garlic, crushed
1	bay leaf, crumbled or cut
½-1	teaspoon tarragon
½-1	teaspoon savory
2	teaspoon salt

Preheat oven to 350°F. Wash and prepare vegetables. Place vegetables in 9 X 13 inch baking dish. (They should be mixed, not layered). In saucepan, heat the bouillon with oil, garlic, bay, savory, tarragon and salt to the boiling point. Pour over vegetables; cover tightly with a lid or tin foil. Bake 1-1¼ hours, stirring once or twice. Makes 6-8 servings.

(Don't stint on seasonings and don't cook too long, vegetables should still be crisp and have a lot of their original color. Don't lift the lid too often. You can add other vegetables or substitute vegetables, but don't change the seasonings).

Ann S. Langlitz

After 40 years as wife of an Episcopal priest and hundreds of parish suppers, I cannot bear to look at lasagna, scalloped potatoes or green bean casseroles. But there were some great wine tasting parties along the way to compensate. This dish travels well, looks good and always is a success.

stick shuttle

Josie Utley, "Fantasy Boa," 83", woven of black mohair, wool, acrylic and velour highlighted by multicolor and gold novelty yarns, 1992.

ZUCCHINI ITALIANO-GRECO

2	tablespoons olive oil
3	large cloves of garlic, cut up
1	pound lean ground beef
1	teaspoon salt
½	teaspoon pepper
2	teaspoons oregano
1	oversized zucchini, 12 X 4 inches, cut into 1 inch cubes
1	large white onion, sliced
1	6 ounce can tomato paste
1 1/8	cup water or bouillon
6	ounces Mozzarella cheese, coarsely chopped
2	tablespoons parsley, finely chopped

Preheat oven to 350°F. Sauté garlic in olive oil for 2 minutes and place in 3 quart casserole. Add crumbled ground beef to skillet; sauté until brown. Transfer to the casserole with the garlic. Sprinkle with ½ the salt, pepper and oregano. Rapidly sauté the zucchini cubes. Do not over-cook. Place in a layer on top meat and repeat the seasonings. Sauté onion rings and place on zucchini. Dissolve tomato paste with 1 1/8 cups water or bouillon and pour over all. Cover with Mozzarella pieces and parsley. Bake uncovered until zucchini is al dente and dish is bubbly - approximately ½-3/4 hour.

Josie

Josie Utley

Most weavers love to cook, and many have vegetable gardens. I designed this recipe to meet the problem of keeping up with the inordinate growth of zucchini and produce a delicious and inexpensive casserole at the same time. It can easily be doubled or tripled.

GRANDMA ALICE'S STUFFED CABBAGE

Sauce:
2 32 ounce cans whole tomatoes,
    chopped, liquid reserved
1 can tomato soup
2 12 ounce cans tomato paste
3 tablespoons dark brown sugar
1 lemon
2 yellow onions, chopped (optional)
    salt to taste
    golden raisins
Filling:
    juice of 1 lemon
3 tablespoons white rice, uncooked
3 tablespoons dark brown sugar
2 pounds ground beef
1 yellow onion, grated (optional)
    salt and pepper to taste
2 whole eggs, beaten
3 tablespoons cold water
2 large heads white cabbage

To make sauce: In medium saucepan, combine tomatoes with juice,
soup, tomato paste, brown sugar, lemon juice, onions, salt and raisins.
Cook 10 minutes over medium heat.
To make filling: In large bowl, mix lemon juice, rice, brown sugar
and beef. Add onion, salt, pepper, eggs and water to meat mixture.
To prepare cabbage (there are 3 methods to soften cabbage for rolling):
1) Freeze the whole cabbage 1 day before use, then defrost. 2) Steam
the whole cabbage for 10 minutes - do not over-cook. 3) Par boil
whole cabbage for 5 minutes - do not over-cook. Once the cabbage is
soft, remove leaves and slice around the heavy membrane and remove.
(Chop remaining cabbage coarsely for bottom of pan when cooking.)

Place 1 large tablespoon meat filling in center at edge of 1 leaf cabbage and wrap tightly, folding over edges and rolling to completely enclose meat. In a large Dutch oven or stock pot, place chopped cabbage evenly over bottom of pan with enough sauce to cover. Place rolled, filled cabbage leaves carefully into pan with seam down, and slowly pour sauce over cabbage, not to disturb rolls. Cook at low temperature on top of stove for 2 hours. (You want the sauce to be both sweet and sour. Add more sugar or lemon juice to your liking.) This dish can be cooked a day ahead to allow the cabbage rolls to absorb a richer flavor from the sauce. If cooled, skim off any fat from sauce.

Sari

Sari Susan Kaplan

My grandmother cooked this on Jewish holidays when I was a child. The New Year was a very special time; sweet foods were made for a sweet year. Cooking her special recipes always makes me think of her and all her love.

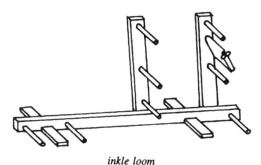

inkle loom

105

Sari Susan Kaplan, rug, wool, boundweave in shades of pink, blue, and grey, 1982; basket, dyed reed, 1992.

ZUCCHINI HERB CASSEROLE

1½	pounds zucchini
2	tablespoon salad oil
1	cup green onion, sliced
1	clove garlic, minced
2	medium tomatoes, seeded and chopped
1¼	teaspoon garlic salt
½	teaspoon basil
½	teaspoon paprika
½	teaspoon oregano
1	cup white or brown rice, cooked
2	cups sharp cheese, shredded

Preheat oven to 350°F. Cut zucchini into ¼ inch slices. Heat oil in a large frying pan over medium low heat. Stir in zucchini, onion and garlic. Cover and cook 5-7 minutes or until vegetables are barely tender when pierced. Remove pan from heat and mix in tomatoes, garlic salt, basil, oregano, paprika and rice. Add 1 cup cheese. Spoon mixture into a shallow 1½ quart baking dish. Sprinkle with the remaining cheese. Chill if made ahead. Bake uncovered for 25 minutes or 35 minutes if dish is cold. Cheese should be bubbly. Let stand 5 minutes before serving.

Valerie

Valerie L. Day

Recipe adapted from <u>Sunset</u> Magazine September 1976.

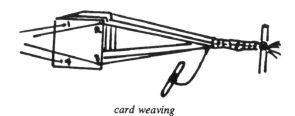

card weaving

Molly Petram, dress with coat, silk, woven in shades of rose, orange and lavender with inlays of rayon and metallics, 1992.

MUSHROOM ARTICHOKE CASSEROLE

1   10 ounce package frozen artichoke
     hearts or 8½ ounce canned artichokes (not
     marinated)
1   pound fresh medium mushrooms, washed,
     trimmed and halved or quartered
½   cup green onions, with tops, sliced
4   tablespoon margarine
2   tablespoons all-purpose flour
     salt and pepper to taste
3/4 cup water
¼   cup milk
1   chicken bouillon cube or
     1 teaspoon chicken bouillon granules
1   teaspoon lemon juice
1/8 teaspoon nutmeg
3/4 cup bread crumbs
1   tablespoon margarine or butter

Preheat oven to 350°F. Cook artichokes in medium sauce pan of
boiling water for 8 minutes. Drain and set aside. (If using canned
artichokes, drain and quarter). Sauté mushrooms and onions with
margarine in a large skillet. Remove vegetables from skillet and stir
in flour, salt and pepper. Add milk, water, bouillon, lemon juice and
nutmeg. Stir until bubbly over low heat. Return mushrooms and
onions to skillet and add artichokes. Bring to simmer, stirring to mix.
Turn into a greased 1 quart casserole dish. In medium bowl, combine
bread crumbs and margarine and sprinkle around edge. Bake for 20
minutes. Make 4-6 servings.

Molly

Molly Petram

Josie Utley, "Kitchen God," 20" X 5", wools, double weave sampler in shades of blues, browns, pinks and yellows, 1977.

"O POLLO MIO" or CHICKEN MY STYLE

2	split Cornish game hens
1	tablespoon oregano, crushed
1	tablespoon cayenne
2	teaspoon salt
1	teaspoon pepper
1	tablespoon olive oil
¼-½	cup Vermouth
1	white onion, cut in large squares
1	red onion, cut in large squares
1	bell pepper, cut in large squares
2	fresh tomatoes, cut in large squares

Preheat oven to 350°F. Place game hens, bone side down, in a shallow ovenproof baking dish. Mix oregano, cayenne, salt, pepper in a small bowl. Sprinkle ½ of the seasonings and drizzle olive oil over the game hens. Bake ½ hour or until they have puffed and browned some. Taking dish out of oven, place onions, bell pepper, and tomatoes around game hens. Sprinkle vegetables with remaining seasonings and olive oil. Add Vermouth, making sure there is sufficient to keep moisture in the bottom of the pan. Return dish to oven and continue cooking until birds are done but vegetables are not overcooked, approximately 45 minutes to 1 hour. Baste with juices several times during cooking period. Makes 4 servings.

Josie

Josie Utley

The name is a take-off on the familiar Italian song "O Sole Mio" but the dish is really more hispanic in its seasonings. It is an original creation.

111

SIMPLY CHICKEN

4-6 chicken thighs
1   10 3/4 ounce can chicken broth, or
       1 14½ ounce can Swanson's clear
       chicken broth
¼   cup water

(Results are best when cooked in an electric skillet.) Skin and remove all fat from the chicken thighs. Pour about ½ of the broth into the skillet; set to simmer. Place thighs in the broth, bone side down. Cook for about 30 minutes or until tender. About half way through the cooking time, turn the thighs (use tongs), so the meaty side is down. Watch carefully when the broth is almost reduced, and add water if pan seems too dry. Cook until the broth is completely reduced and the chicken is a deep gold, moist and rich. There should be no liquid left in the pan. Skinned breasts can be prepared this same way, but will require a little more broth or water to remain moist.

Jean

Jean Wilson

To cut down on fat, calories, and preparation time, I devised this simple way to cook chicken thighs in broth. The flavor is pure chicken and stands alone. Let your accompaniment - pilaf, noodles, salad or vegetables - add any extra tastes.

112

OYSTER SAUCE CHICKEN

2	frying chickens, cut up
½-3/4	cup oyster sauce
½	cup sherry
2	tablespoons Dijon-style mustard
1	tablespoons fresh ginger, minced
1	cup water
2-5	drops sesame oil
½	yellow onion, minced, or
	1 tablespoon dry chopped onion
1/8	teaspoon ground white pepper
2-3	tablespoons soy sauce
2	garlic cloves, minced

Preheat oven to 350°F. Arrange cut up chicken pieces in a 13 X 9 inch shallow baking dish. In a separate bowl, combine oyster sauce, sherry, mustard, ginger, water, sesame oil, onion, pepper, soy sauce and garlic; mix well. Pour sauce over chicken. Cover tightly with foil and bake for about 1 hour (or bake at 325°F for 2 hours for frozen chicken). When chicken is cooked, remove foil, increase heat to 400°F, and return chicken to oven. Baste every 10 minutes until sauce has thickened and dried somewhat (20-30 minutes). Makes 6 servings.

Polly

Polly Zetterberg

This dish works great for dinners after soccer practice, swimming lessons, looms that won't let go of you, and other items that call you from the kitchen at dinner prep time. Serve with steamed white rice and steamed brocolli. Encourage folks to drizzle the remaining sauce over their rice and brocolli. It's my kids' favorite meal.

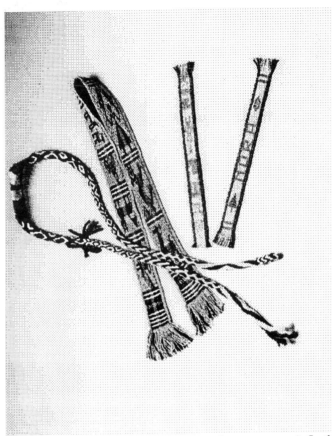

Sue Bichsel, bookmark, belt, slings, rayons and cottons, woven in South American braiding, Intermesh, Bolivian Pebbleweave, and Andean sling techniques, 1987.

MARCO POLO CHICKEN BREASTS

1 cup red wine
¼ cup soy sauce
¼ cup salad oil
2 tablespoons water
1 clove garlic, peeled and sliced
1 teaspoon powdered ginger
¼ teaspoon oregano
1 tablespoon brown sugar, packed
4 chicken breast halves
3-4 cups rice, cooked (brown or white)

Preheat oven to 375°F. Combine red wine, soy sauce, oil, water, garlic, ginger, oregano and brown sugar in a bowl, mixing well. Place chicken breasts in a large casserole dish. Pour sauce over chicken and cover. Bake 1½ hours, uncovering for last 15 minutes. Place chicken on mound of cooked rice and pour sauce over all.

Sue

Sue Bichsel

I call this "Marco Polo" Chicken Breasts because the flavors are a blend of two cuisines - soy sauce and ginger from China and wine and garlic from Italy. It was served to me during a trip to New Mexico (of all places), and it reminds me of the many threads that come together in cooking and in weaving.

Virginia I. Harvey, tapestry, 5" X 4", silk soumak on bamboo frame, woven in shades of olive greens and greys, 1992.

CACHE-VEY (CASH-WAY)

4	tablespoons oil
4	tablespoons all-purpose flour
2	cups chicken stock or broth
2	cups cooked chicken or turkey meat
	(canned or left-overs are acceptable)
	salt and pepper to taste
1½	teaspoon curry powder (as desired)
1½	cups rice, cooked

optional condiments:
    cabbage, shredded
    raisins
    crushed pineapple
    peanuts
    celery, sliced
    sesame seeds, toasted
    tomato, sliced
    cucumber, sliced
    cheese, grated
    green and/or red bell pepper
    Mandarin oranges
    shoe string potatoes

Heat oil and blend in flour. Slowly stir in chicken stock or broth. Cook and stir until thickened. Add meat, salt, pepper, and curry powder. Boil rice according to package directions. Serve chicken over rice and let each add condiments as he/she wishes.

Barbara

Barbara Mahan

This is a fun feast for children or guests of unknown tastes. With so many side dishes, nobody is left out. My children thought the shoestring potatoes were the most important topping.

117

Valerie L. Day, assorted Christmas and greeting cards, 5½" X 4¼", wools, woven in twill and inset in colored folded paper, 1984.

BBQ RIBS

8 pounds country style pork spareribs
¼ cup flour
2 cups tomato juice
1 cup water
1 cup cider vinegar
2 onions, chopped fine
1 cup celery, chopped
½ teaspoon ground ginger
½ teaspoon cayenne pepper
2 cups sugar
4 tablespoons butter or margarine
2 cloves garlic
1 teaspoon salt
½ teaspoon nutmeg
1 teaspoon paprika

Preheat oven to 325°F. Cover spareribs with water and boil in a covered roasting pan 1 hour to make plump and to remove fat. Drain the water; leave ribs in the pan. In medium bowl, mix the flour and ¼ cup tomato juice to make a paste. Add remaining juice. Add water, vinegar, onions, celery, ginger, cayenne, sugar, butter, garlic, salt, nutmeg and paprika and mix well. Pour over the ribs. Bake 4 hours. Serve over hot rice. (Freezes well.) Makes 8 servings.

Valerie

Valerie L. Day

My sister's favorite dish to take to a potluck, as it feeds a crowd. For my own family, I make half a recipe.

119

Irene Ohannesian, jacket, wool, woven in shades of grey and blue, front patchwork in purples, greens and rust inspired by Seminole piecing techniques, 1988.

SHEPHERD'S PIE

1 pound ground round
1 medium onion, chopped
2 tablespoons Worcestershire sauce
 salt and pepper to taste
½ cup stock or water
1 10 ounce package frozen peas
2 cups mashed potatoes
2 tablespoons butter

Preheat oven to 350°F. Brown meat in skillet with onion, Worcestershire sauce, salt and pepper. Add stock (or water) to meat mixture stirring to form a nice brown gravy. Add peas. Place meat mixture into 9 inch pie pan. Top with mashed potatoes and drizzle with butter all over top. Bake for 30 minutes.

Irene

Irene Ohannesian

Shepherd's Pie, like all standard English fare, is meant to be changed by using available supplies or "left-overs" and the creativity of the cook.

GOULASH WITH CARAWAY SEEDS

3   pounds sirloin tip or rump roast, cut into one
     inch cubes, trimmed of fat and gristle
1   tablespoon cooking oil
2   cups onion, chopped
1   teaspoon caraway seeds
     salt to taste
½   cup water
¼   cup catsup
1   tablespoon paprika
     pasta, cooked
     potatoes, boiled
     eggs, hard boiled, sliced, to garnish

In large skillet, sauté cut beef cubes on all sides in oil, for 5 minutes.
Remove meat from skillet and add onions and more oil if necessary.
Sauté 5 minutes, stirring. Return beef to skillet and add caraway
seeds, salt and water. Bring to simmer. Cook, covered, for about 1
hour or until tender, adding more water if needed. Mix catsup and
paprika with 2 tablespoons liquid from beef mixture in small bowl.
Stir sauce into stew and simmer 10 minutes more. Serve over pasta or
boiled potatoes. (Garnish with hard boiled egg slices if desired.)
Makes 6 servings.

Melba

Melba Short

"Good enough to serve to guests."

122

NORWEGIAN MEAT BALLS

1 pound ground round
½ pound ground pork or Jimmy Dean pork sausage
1 large whole egg
½ cup bread crumbs, fresh or dried
¼ cup Parmesan cheese
1 medium onion, grated
½ teaspoon soy sauce
½ teaspoon Tabasco sauce
½ teaspoon Worcestershire sauce
½ teaspoon dried sweet basil
½ teaspoon Accent
½ teaspoon allspice
½ teaspoon garlic powder
½ teaspoon salt
½ teaspoon freshly ground pepper
2 tablespoon margarine
  all-purpose flour for coating
1 beef bouillon cube
1 cup hot water

Mix ground round, ground pork, egg, breadcrumbs, cheese, onion, soy sauce, Tabasco, Worcestershire, basil, Accent, allspice, garlic powder, salt and pepper in medium bowl, mixing thoroughly with spoon or hands. Form into 1¼ inch balls. Roll in flour and sauté balls in margarine in large skillet, browning on all sides. In small bowl, add bouillon cube to hot water and add to skillet. Simmer, covered ½ hour. Makes 25-30 balls.

Inger

Inger Osberg

I always double this recipe which I have had for 38 years so I can spend more time at the loom or spinning wheel. Enjoy!

BEEF STROGANOFF

¼ cup butter
¼ cup onion, chopped
1 clove garlic, minced
2 3 ounce cans mushrooms, drained
1 pound ground beef
3 tablespoons lemon juice
3 tablespoons Burgundy wine
1 can condensed consomme
1 teaspoon salt
¼ teaspoon pepper
¼ pound medium noodles, uncooked
1 cup sour cream

Sauté onions, mushrooms and garlic in butter. Add beef and cook until redness is gone. Add lemon juice, Burgundy, consomme, salt and pepper to mixture. Simmer uncovered for 15 minutes. Stir in uncooked noodles. Cook covered until noodles are tender. Add sour cream and heat throughout. Do not boil. Makes 6 servings.

Kay Schrader

CHILI VARIATIONS

Walnut chili:
1   cup walnut meats, coarsely chopped

Hazelnut chili:
1   cup hazelnut meats, coarsely chopped

Mushroom chili:
1-2   cups hearty "beefsteak" mushrooms,
        chopped in large pieces (i.e.
        chanterelles, boletes, or meadows)
        that won't "disappear" in the cooking

Cilantro chili:
½-3/4 cups cilantro, chopped, added in
        the last ½ hour of simmering

Garlic chili:
8-10   whole garlic cloves, peeled
        (they're easy to pick out for
        those who won't eat them)

Ingredients can be in addition to or instead of the meat. Measurements are for a 2 quart pot of chili. Add variations after the beans are thoroughly cooked.

Mary Beth

Mary Beth Rawlins

As the weather gets cooler in the fall, and I'm putting larger winter projects on my loom, I begin to remember how much I love a pot of chili. Besides tasting good, I like to have a hearty, ready-made lunch that's quick and easy and will help keep me "beating the loom" all afternoon long.

CAMACHO

1   pound lean ground beef
1   Bermuda-type onion, finely chopped
2   16 ounce cans Rosarita refried beans
1   cup black olives, diced
2   tomatoes, chopped
1-2 dashes hot sauce
1   pound Jack cheese, grated
    salt and pepper to taste
Optional:
1   8 ounce can tomato sauce, if you want
    it juicier
    corn tortillas, heated

Saute the beef until brown; drain fat. Add onion; stir and brown. Add beans, olives, tomatoes, hot sauce, salt and pepper and stir. Add optional tomato sauce here if you think you need it. Add cheese and stir until well mixed and stringy. Pile on top of hot tortillas. Makes 6 servings.

SyLVIA

Sylvia Tacker

We followed a dry, dusty road cutting across rusting railroad tracks to the best Mexican restaurant on the Mexicalli border. The faded sign on the outside of the galvanized metal building said "Camacho's". The food was great. Camach, the half-Irish proprietor, sat in front of the only fan and beamed at everyone. We never saw him do anything except drink Pepsi and talk, but from his bulk, he had not missed any meals. Senora Camacho did all the cooking, making her own beans and tortillas. As a friend of ours once said, this recipe "looks terrible, but boy, does it taste good!"

PHAD THAI

8 ounces thin rice noodles
1½ cups fresh bean sprouts
1 bunch scallions, chopped
3 tablespoons sesame oil
1 tablespoon chili garlic paste
2 tablespoons paprika
3 tablespoons fish sauce
1 tablespoon soy sauce
3 tablespoons granulated sugar
5 tablespoons water
2 whole eggs, lightly scrambled
3 tablespoons peanuts, chopped
3 cups cooked meat (chicken, pork,
   beef, shrimp or tofu)
   purple cabbage, shredded
   carrots, shredded
   been sprouts

Soak rice noodles in hot water to cover for about 30 minutes; drain. Sauté bean sprouts and scallions (save some of the tops for garnish) with oil in a large skillet or wok. Mix chili paste, paprika, fish sauce, soy sauce, sugar, and water in small bowl. Add noodles to skillet. Add sauce mixture and cooked meat; toss with noodles. Add scrambled egg and nuts (save some nuts for garnish). Serve on a bed of sprouts, purple cabbage and carrots, topped with saved scallions and more nuts. Makes 6 servings. (You can get the chili paste, fish sauce sesame oil and rice noodles in most Asian markets. This is mildly hot to me; you can adjust by adding more or less chili garlic paste.)

Gwen Zierdt

127

Sumar Studios, blanket, 69" x 43", wool, mohair, rayon, and metallics, woven in plain weave in shades of purple and periwinkle, 1991.

MOM'S TERIYAKI SAUCE

½   cup soy sauce (Kikkoman brand)
1   tablespoon fresh ginger, grated
1   clove garlic, crushed
2   tablespoons brown sugar
¼   cup dry sherry

Mix soy sauce, ginger, garlic, brown sugar and sherry in small bowl. Use this sauce when making teriyaki chicken, pork, beef and fish. Makes 1 cup.

Marcy

Marcy Johnson

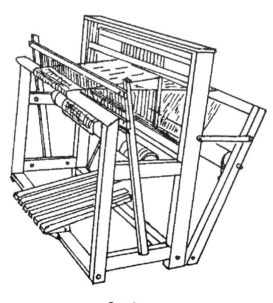

floor loom

Sweets

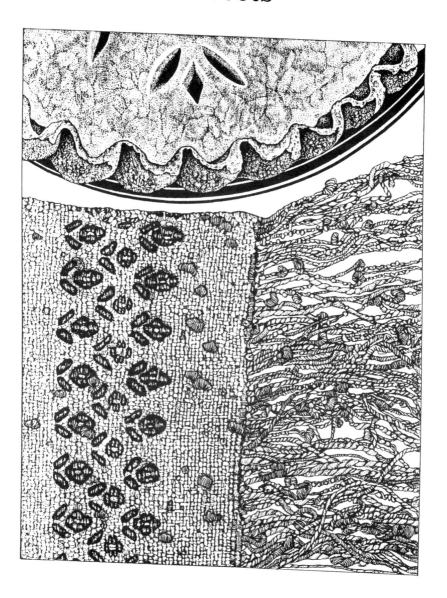

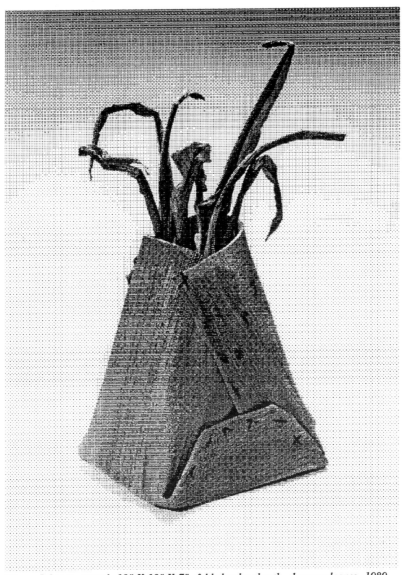

Marcy Johnson, vessel, 18" X 10" X 7", folded palm sheath, dracena leaves, 1989.

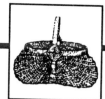

LARGE GOOEY
CHOCOLATE CHIP COOKIES

1½	cup shortening
1½	cup brown sugar, packed
3/4	cup granulated sugar
1½	teaspoon vanilla extract
½	teaspoon salt
3	whole eggs, beaten
3	teaspoons baking soda
4	tablespoons hot water
5-6	cups all-purpose flour, sifted
1	12 ounce package semi-sweet chocolate chips
1	cup pecans or walnuts, chopped

Preheat oven to 350°F. In mixing bowl, cream shortening, sugars and salt thoroughly. Add vanilla and eggs. Dissolve soda in water in small bowl. Add soda water to shortening and mix well after each addition. Add flour, enough so that dough does not stick to fingers when touched, or until it pulls away from sides of bowl when mixing. Add chocolate chips and nuts. Dough will be thick. Bake on ungreased cookie sheets for 9-11 minutes. It's a poor cookie that won't grease it's own bottom! Let stand a few moments then remove to racks or plates to cool. Makes 5-6 dozen.

Marcy

Marcy Johnson

Make large cookies so you can say, "I only had one!"

DOUBLE CHOCOLATE CHIP COOKIES

1	cup quick uncooked oats, ground fine in blender
2½	cups all-purpose flour
1½	teaspoons baking powder
1	teaspoon baking soda
¼	teaspoon salt
1	cup dark chocolate chips
1	cup plus 5 tablespoons unsalted butter
1	cup packed light brown sugar
1/3	cup granulated sugar
2	whole eggs
2½	teaspoons vanilla extract
2	cups white chocolate chips

Preheat oven to 350°. Mix oats, flour, baking powder, baking soda and salt in medium bowl. Melt the dark chocolate chips in a double boiler. Cream sugars and butter together in mixing bowl until fluffy. Add eggs and vanilla. Beat in melted chocolate. Add dry ingredients and white chocolate chips gradually until well mixed. Refrigerate dough until firm, about 20-30 minutes. Shape dough into walnut sized balls and place on ungreased baking sheet. Bake 9-11 minutes until just firm. Do NOT over-bake--they will still be soft right out of the oven. Let stand on baking sheet 3-4 minutes and then cool cookies on wire racks. Makes 2 dozen cookies.

Gwen Zierdt

My husband's family has nicknamed these cookies 'Chocolate Bombs'!

OATMEAL COOKIES

1	cup margarine
1	cup brown sugar, packed
1	cup granulated sugar
2	whole eggs
1½	cups all-purpose flour
1	teaspoon soda
1	teaspoon salt
1	teaspoon vanilla
3	cups uncooked oats, old fashioned
1	cup raisins

Preheat oven to 400°F. Cream margarine; add sugars and beat until light. Add eggs and continue beating. Sift together flour, soda and salt and add to margarine mixture in stages. Stir vanilla, oatmeal and raisins until blended. Drop by tablespoons onto ungreased cookie sheet. Bake for 10 minutes. Makes 3 dozen.

Variations: Add 1 cup chocolate chips, coconut or nuts in addition to or to replace raisins.

(I've substituted Egg Beaters, omitted nuts and cut down on shortening for my husband's low fat diet, but they are not as good.)

Mary Nolting

Carry these cookies in the car when you are on a long trip with kids. They will settle empty stomachs and quiet everyone down if you still have an hour or so to go before stopping for supper.

Tomoe Edwards, "Dancers in Damask," 17" X 14", ecru and black cottons, woven in damask satin technique, framed, 1992.

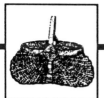

OATMEAL AND NUT COOKIES

1¼   cups margarine
3/4   cup firmly packed brown sugar
3/4   cup granulated sugar
1   whole egg
1   teaspoon vanilla
1½   cups all-purpose flour
1   teaspoon baking soda
1   teaspoon salt
1   teaspoon cinnamon
2½   cups uncooked oats, quick or old fashioned
1   cup walnuts

Preheat oven to 375°F. Beat margarine and sugars until fluffy. Beat in egg and vanilla. Add combined flour, baking soda, salt and cinnamon. Mix well. Stir in oatmeal and nuts. Drop by rounded teaspoonfuls onto ungreased cookie sheet. Bake 10-11 minutes. Makes 4½ dozen cookies.

Tomoe

Tomoe Edwards

Recipe adapted from one appearing on Quick Quaker Oats box.

beginning a
base

137

HAROLD'S OATMEAL COOKIES

1   cup all-purpose flour
1   teaspoon baking soda
½   teaspoon salt
½   teaspoon ground cinnamon
1   cup butter, softened
3/4 cup granulated sugar
3/4 cup brown sugar, packed
2   whole eggs
1   teaspoon vanilla
3   cups uncooked oats, old fashioned
1   small package chocolate morsels
½   cup raisins (soak overnight and drain)
1   cup walnuts or pecans, chopped

Preheat oven to 375°F. In a small bowl, combine flour, baking soda, salt and cinnamon; set aside. In a large bowl, combine butter, sugars, eggs and vanilla; beat until creamy. Gradually add flour mixture. Stir in oats, chocolate morsels, raisins and nuts. Drop by rounded tablespoons onto ungreased cookie sheet. Bake for 8-10 minutes or until golden brown. Makes 4-5 dozen 3 inch cookies.

SyLVIA

Sylvia Tacker
In memory of Harold Tacker

Harold Tacker joined the Seattle Weavers' Guild in 1973, served on its board in several capacities and gave mini-workshops in twining and photography. He hosted the bulletin assembly for a year in his studio. These cookies came to many lunchtime events at the Guild.

138

JAY'S OATMEAL COOKIES

1	cup margarine
1	cup brown sugar, packed
1	cup granulated sugar
2	whole eggs
1	teaspoon vanilla extract
4	cups uncooked oats, old fashioned
1½	cups all-purpose flour
1	cup chocolate chips
½	cup wheat germ
1	cup walnuts or pecans, chopped
1	teaspoon baking soda

Preheat oven to 350°F. In large mixing bowl, cream margarine with sugars. Add eggs and vanilla. Beat well. Mix together the oatmeal, flour, chocolate chips, wheat germ, nuts and baking soda in another bowl, then add to the butter mixture. Mix thoroughly. This is a stiff dough. Make dough into balls whatever size you want and flatten with a fork or a bottom of glass. Jay makes them big and fat. Place on lightly buttered cookie sheets and cook for 8-10 minutes. Watch them closely. They are done when slightly golden brown. Cool and store in a cookie tin or heavy ziplock bags. Makes about 3 dozen.

Martha

Martha Cram

Jay is a long time ski friend who is also an orthodontist. Cookies are only a small part of his culinary skills. These cookies are particularly sturdy and travel well to picnics or in your rucksack.

139

GOLD MEDAL SOFT MOLASSES COOKIES

1 ¼	cup shortening
1	cup granulated sugar
6	cups all-purpose flour
2	teaspoons soda
1	teaspoon salt
1	teaspoon allspice
1	teaspoon ginger
1	teaspoon cinnamon
1	cup dark molasses
1	cup cold coffee
	flour (to roll)

Preheat oven to 350-375°F. In a small bowl, cream shortening and sugar. In large bowl, sift flour and spices. In a third bowl, mix molasses and coffee. Alternate, blending molasses and flour mixtures into the creamed mixture. Chill dough 2-3 hours or overnight. You'll need a little more flour to roll out. Roll at least ¼ inch thick. Cut out circles with a round cookie cutter, 4-5 inches across. This is a satisfying size for teenage boys. Brush cookies with milk (don't be sloppy). Bake on greased cookie sheet for 8-10 minutes. DO NOT OVER-BAKE - they are to be "cake-like". Makes 2-3 dozen, depending on size.

Laurel

Laurel V. Haseley

In 1929, my mother, Violet Cerny, received an oak box filled with recipes for a wedding present. They cost $1.00. At 90 years of age, she still is using many of these recipes, and I've made a gazillion dozen of the molasses cookies.

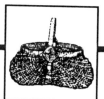

GINGER SNAPS

3/4	cup butter
2	cups granulated sugar
2	whole eggs, well beaten
½	cup molasses
2	teaspoons vinegar
3 3/4	cups all-purpose flour
1½	teaspoons baking soda
2-3	teaspoons powdered ginger
½	teaspoons cinnamon
¼	teaspoons ground cloves

Preheat oven to 325°F. With mixer, cream butter and sugar until light. Stir in eggs, molasses and vinegar. In separate bowl, sift together flour, soda, ginger, cinnamon and cloves; add to butter mixture. Blend the mixture completely with a spoon. Form dough into 3/4 inch balls and place on greased cookie sheet. (Dough may handle better if chilled ahead.) Bake for 12 minutes. Makes 10 dozen.

Special kid treat: Cut marshmallow in half. Place cut side down on almost baked cookies (about 8 minutes done); return to oven for remaining 4 minutes.

Valerie

Valerie L. Day

Adapted from Joy of Cooking, 1964 ed.

SPRITZ BUTTER COOKIES

1	pound butter
1¼	cup granulated sugar
1	teaspoon vanilla
3/4	teaspoon almond extract
2	whole eggs
5	cups all-purpose flour

Preheat oven to 350°F. Cream butter until fluffy. Add sugar, vanilla and almond extract to butter and mix. Add eggs and blend well; blend in flour thoroughly. Fill cookie press with dough and force through. Using the "star" plate, form circles (these may be decorated with candied cherries to make Christmas wreaths or "S"s.) The comb-shaped plate makes long bars on cookie sheet which are cut into individual cookies using a spatula. Bake for 10-12 minutes until edges turn golden brown. Let cool slightly before removing from cookie sheet. Yields about 4 dozen cookies.

Midge

Midge Dodge

These cookies won first prize in a Chicago newspaper contest. The recipe comes from a cookbook compiled by the Sandia Base Women's Club, Albuquerque, New Mexico. The secret is to use real butter (nothing else will do).

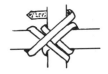

4-point lashing

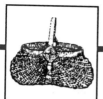

ALMOND BAR COOKIES

1 cup butter
3/4 cup granulated sugar
4 ounces almond paste
1 egg yolk, plus
   1 egg white
1 teaspoon almond extract
2 cups all-purpose flour, sifted
½ cup almonds, slivered

Preheat 350°F. Cream butter, sugar and almond paste together. Add egg yolk, almond extract and flour. Mix well and spread into buttered 8 inch springform or cake pan. Beat egg white until stiff. Spread over batter mixture. Sprinkle with almonds. Bake 30 minutes until golden brown. Best if made a day in advance. Cool and cut into bars. Makes about 2 dozen cookies.

Joanne

Joanne McConnell

These cookies are wonderful and easy to make for a crowd.

plaited weave

143

Gillian Bull, jacket, wool and cotton, machine knit in shades of fuchsia, purple, black and tangerine, 1992.

ANZAC BISCUITS
(my first New Zealand cookie recipe)

1 cup granulated sugar
6 ounces margarine
1 tablespoon light molasses
1 cup coconut, flaked or grated
1 cup uncooked oats, quick
1 cup all-purpose flour
1 teaspoon baking powder
1 cup chopped peanuts or peanut butter

Preheat oven to 325°F. Melt sugar, margarine and molasses in small sauce pan. Add remaining ingredients and mix well. Pour batter into a 15 X 10 X 1 inch greased jelly roll pan, to make a ¼ inch thick layer (or drop by spoonfuls to make single cookies). Bake for 15-20 minutes. Let cool 10 minutes then cut apart. (This is a very flexible recipe, and since I don't measure very accurately, it comes out differently each time, but it is always good.)

Gillian

Gillian Bull

After I had been weaving for 2 years, we returned to New Zealand for a visit. I met some wonderful weavers and spinners. One weaver in particular made a big difference to my feelings about weaving. She said that she couldn't wait to finish the present project and dress the loom for the next one; I commented that I dreaded threading the loom and tended to put off starting the next piece. She drew herself up, looked me in the eye, and said, "How can you call yourself a weaver and not like to dress the loom?" Pow, I had better change my attitude fast. I did. I even learned to enjoy dressing the loom, though I never used more than 20 ends per inch, and now I knit.

SUGAR COOKIES

2	cups all-purpose flour
1½	teaspoon baking powder
¼	teaspoon salt
2/3	cup shortening
1	teaspoon vanilla
3/4	cup granulated sugar
1	tablespoon brown sugar, packed
½	teaspoon nutmeg
1	whole egg, whipped
1	tablespoon milk

Preheat oven to 375°F. In a large mixing, bowl sift flour, baking powder and salt. In a separate bowl, mix shortening, vanilla, sugars and nutmeg. Cream all together until smooth. Whip egg until light; add milk and blend thoroughly into previous mixture. Cover with clean towel and refrigerate for 1 hour; dough will be very stiff. Roll out dough to 3/16 inch. Cut out cookies and place onto baking sheet. Allow space between, as they will spread. Sprinkle cookies with sugar. Bake for 8-10 minutes.

Lynn

Lynn Heglar

While you're baking these sugar cookies, put a pot of coffee on the stove, finish weaving those beautiful napkins you've always wanted and fan yourself with a weaving magazine so you'll be fresh and cool when company arrives.

SOUR CREAM TWISTS

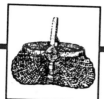

4   cups all-purpose flour
½   teaspoon salt
½   cup butter
½   cup shortening
2   packages dry yeast
¼   cup warm water
1   cup sour cream
1   whole egg, plus
2   egg yolks, well beaten
1   teaspoon vanilla
1   cup granulated sugar (or more for
     sprinkling on dough and board)

Preheat oven to 350°F. Sift flour and salt into a bowl. Cut in shortening to form a coarse meal. Dissolve the yeast in ¼ cup warm water. Let stand 5 minutes. Add yeast, beaten eggs, sour cream and vanilla to flour mixture. Mix thoroughly by hand; dough will be stiff. Cover with damp cloth and place in refrigerator for 2-3 hours. Divide dough into thirds. Roll out each 1/3 on sugar-sprinkled board. Sprinkle with sugar and fold in thirds. Repeat 2 more times. Roll dough into a rectangle 4 X 14 inches. Cut strips 1 inch wide and 4 inches long. Twist. Place on greased pans and let rise 45 minutes. Bake 18-20 minutes until very light brown. Makes 36 twists.

Mary Jo

Mary Jo Aegerter

A much loved family recipe. We got it from an Iowa grandmother.

NANAIMO BARS

½ cup butter or margarine
5 tablespoons unsweetened cocoa
¼ cup granulated sugar
1 whole egg, beaten
1 teaspoon vanilla
2 cups graham crackers, crumbled
1 cup coconut, finely grated
¼ cup butter or margarine
2 tablespoons Bird's Custard Powder
2 tablespoons hot water
2 cups powdered sugar
4 squares semi-sweet chocolate, melted

In the top of a double boiler, add the butter, cocoa, sugar, egg and vanilla. Stir over hot water until the butter melts and the mixture thickens a little, to resemble custard. Remove from heat. In a bowl, combine the graham cracker crumbs and coconut. Add to the custard mixture in the double boiler and blend thoroughly. Press into a greased 9 inch square pan. Refrigerate. Blend butter, custard powder mixed with water and powdered sugar into a smooth icing. Let cool a little and spread on top of the cocoa base. Melt the chocolate over hot water and spread over icing. Refrigerate. Slice into bars. Makes 9 bars.

In memory of
Helen Ingraham

This recipe was contributed by Nellie Johnston to the SWG SAMPLE PAGES of the Newsletter. It makes a rich addition to the potluck table.

CONGO BARS

2/3	cup margarine
16	ounces brown sugar, packed
3	whole eggs
½	teaspoon salt
2 2/3	cups all-purpose flour
2½	teaspoons baking power
1	6 ounce package semi-sweet chocolate chips
½	cups pecans or walnuts, chopped
1	teaspoon vanilla

Preheat oven to 350°F. Melt margarine in small sauce pan. In mixing bowl, beat eggs and add cooled sugar mixture. Mix salt, flour, and baking powder in another bowl and add to sugar mixture. Stir in chips, nuts and vanilla. Press evenly into 15 X 10 X 1 inch teflon or Pam sprayed jelly roll pan. Bake 30 minutes. Cool and cut into squares. Like the Toll House bars, but better!

Gail

Gail Layman

Thirty two years ago in my college days, the mother of a friend always sent these cookies to raise our spirits. They were a favorite then and continue to be tops with my family.

Linda C. Smith, coverlet, 96" X 36", wool woven in overshot in the snails, trails and catpaws pattern, 1978; two pine needle baskets, 5" and 4", 1992.

PEACH SHORTBREAD

½   cup light brown sugar
1   cup all-purpose flour
1/3 cup butter, cold
3/4 cup peaches, dried
     water
2   teaspoons lemon juice
2/3 cup sugar
2   teaspoons cornstarch
½   cup walnuts

Preheat over to 350°F. Combine flour and brown sugar. Cut in butter until crumbly. Press into the bottom of a 8 X 8 inch baking pan. Bake 12 minutes. Cool completely. Meanwhile, place peaches in a saucepan. Cover with water and simmer 15 minutes. Drain peaches; reserve liquid. Chop peaches finely. Return to saucepan with ¼ cup reserved liquid; add lemon juice, sugar and cornstarch. Bring to a boil. Boil 1 minute, stirring constantly. Remove from heat. Cool 10 minutes; spread over crust. Sprinkle with nuts. Bake 20 minutes. Cool and cut into bars. Makes 1 dozen bars.

Linda

Linda C. Smith

151

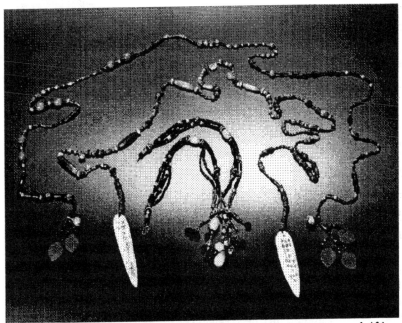

Kathy Dannerbeck, necklaces, metal, glass, semi-precious, bone, stone and African trade beads, 72" (2) 1990; 28" multistrand, 1991.

JERRI'S CREAM CHEESE PIE

1   8 ounce package cream cheese
1   cup powdered sugar
¼   teaspoon vanilla
1   cup whipping cream, whipped
1   pre-made graham cracker pie crust
2   cups blueberries, raspberries or Seattle
      blackberries, frozen
½   cup granulated sugar
1-2 tablespoons cornstarch
up to 1 tablespoon water, if needed

In a food processor, blend cream cheese until smooth and add sugar
and vanilla. In a separate bowl, whip whipping cream and fold into
cream cheese mixture. Spoon mixture into crust, making a slight
indentation in the center for a berry topping. In a medium sauce pan
stir berries and sugar over medium heat until berries soften and sugar
dissolves. Add cornstarch mixed with water to form a smooth paste,
add to berry mixture and simmer. As the berries melt, they mix with
the cornstarch and sugar and thicken into a berry topping without
lumps. Some berries may require a small amount of extra water.
Cool topping and spoon over cream cheese mixture. Refrigerate for
several hours.

Kathy

Kathy Dannerbeck

*I met my friend Jerri Crass in Juneau, Alaska. I convinced her to
try hand spinning and to enter her items in the Southeast Alaska
State Fair. She also entered this recipe for an easy, rich, no-bake
pie. Both her pie and her handspun, handknit hat won blue ribbons!*

FRENCH SATIN PIE

½   cup butter or margarine
3/4 cup sugar
2   squares unsweetened chocolate, melted
1   teaspoon vanilla
2   whole eggs
1   8 inch pie shell, prebaked
    whipped topping (garnish)

Cream butter; add sugar, chocolate, vanilla and one egg. Beat 5 minutes, add other egg and beat 5 minutes more. Pour into a baked 8 inch pie shell. Chill several hours. Serve with or without a whipped topping.

M idge

Midge Dodge

From the 1990 Christmas potluck of the Boise Valley Handweavers' Guild, this reliable recipe is included by special request. It sets up well and holds its shape when served. Boise weavers are chocoholics and chocolate items are very popular at their two yearly potluck luncheons.

154

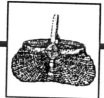

SWISS PLUM PIE

1   crust pie shell, ready made or your
      favorite recipe
24   Italian prune plums, cut in half and
      pitted
¼   cup granulated sugar
1   cup whole milk (in combination with half
      and half if you like a richer pie)
2   whole eggs
¼   cup granulated sugar

Preheat oven to 450°F. Prepare pie crust. Place plums in pie shell cut side up. Sprinkle with ¼ cup sugar and put into oven for 15 minutes. Combine milk, eggs and sugar and whisk until well blended. Pour over the plums and immediately reduce oven temperature to 350°F. Bake 30-40 minutes or until custard looks set. Makes 1 pie.

Sue

Sue Bichsel

I became a Swiss by marriage and so of course I had to learn to make this favorite Swiss dessert. During September, I freeze all my Italian plums in halves so I can make this pie all winter. I have been known to serve it alone for supper. With fruit, eggs and milk it is a complete meal.

Nancy Tracy, fabric samples, 10" x 10", gold and white cotton, woven in Samitum, a Medieval compound twill technique no longer commercially produced, 1992.

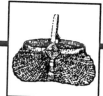

DEEP DISH BERRY PIE

1   3 ounce package cream cheese, softened
6   tablespoons butter, softened
3/4 cups all-purpose flour, sifted
½   teaspoon salt
2   pounds berries (fresh or frozen), thawed
½   cup all-purpose flour
1   cup granulated sugar
½   cup light corn syrup
2   tablespoons butter

Preheat oven to 425°F. Beat cream cheese and butter with mixer until fluffy. Add flour and salt; mix with fork until well blended. Form into a ball with hands. Wrap in waxed paper and chill in refrigerator before rolling. Toss thawed berries with flour and turn into an 8 X 8 X 2 inch baking pan. Sprinkle any left-over flour over berries. In a small saucepan, bring sugar and corn syrup to a boil over medium heat, stirring constantly. Pour liquid over berries and dot with butter. Roll out pastry between two pieces of waxed paper to a size 1 inch larger than baking pan. (This is very sticky dough; do this procedure quickly and try not to warm dough with hands.) Remove top piece of waxed paper. Place pastry over berries with waxed paper side up. Remove and discard waxed paper. Fold edge under and flute double-thickness pastry against the inside edge of pan. Cut several small gashes in center of pastry to let steam escape. Bake 25 minutes. Excellent served with vanilla ice cream.

Nancy

Nancy A. Tracy

PECAN PUMPKIN PIE

1	16 ounce can pumpkin
1	13 ounce can evaporated milk
2	whole eggs
3/4	cup brown sugar, packed
1½	teaspoon cinnamon
½	teaspoon salt
½	teaspoon ginger
½	teaspoon nutmeg
1	9 inch pie shell, unbaked
1	cup whipping cream, whipped (garnish)

Topping:

1	cup walnuts or pecans, chopped
3/4	cup brown sugar, packed
4	tablespoons butter or magarine, melted

Preheat oven to 400°F. Beat pumpkin, milk, brown sugar, cinnamon, salt, ginger and nutmeg with mixer at medium speed until well blended. Pour into prepared pie shell. Bake 40 minutes or until cooked. While cooking, mix nuts, brown sugar and butter in a bowl. Spread topping onto cooked hot pie. Place under broiler 5-7 inches from heat (watch carefully). Broil 3 minutes or until sugar melts. Serve cold and garnish with whipped cream.

Kay

Kay Schrader

APPLE CAKE

½   cup butter
3/4 cup granulated sugar
2   whole eggs
½   teaspoon vanilla extract
1   cup cake flour
2   teaspoons baking powder
4   apples, peeled, quartered and sliced
    juice of ½ lemon
    granulated sugar

Preheat oven to 350°F. Cream together butter and sugar. Add eggs
and vanilla and beat. Blend in flour and baking powder. Butter a 6 X
9½ inch pan or 9 inch pie dish. Fill with batter and top with apples.
Push apples gently into batter; drizzle with lemon juice and sprinkle
with some sugar. Bake for approximately 45-50 minutes. Also good
topped with peaches, apricots, plums or blueberries. Festive when
glazed with 1 cup of heated apricot jam with 1 tablespoon brandy or
liqueur added. Double recipe: use 2 different toppings. Makes 1 cake.

Inge

Inge Buley

*This recipe has been my friend almost as long as weaving has been
my love. Originally a friend from Switzerland shared this recipe with
me and other weavers. In my California weaving days (almost 30
years ago) I could fix this cake while making breakfast for my
children.*

159

GOLD MEDAL INEXPENSIVE SPONGE CAKE

2   whole eggs
½   teaspoon salt
1   cup granulated sugar
1   teaspoon flavoring of choice
½   cup whole milk
1   tablespoon butter
1   cup all-purpose flour, sifted
1   teaspoon baking powder

Preheat oven to 350°F. Beat eggs until very light with electric beater. Blend salt, sugar and flavoring until mixed thoroughly. In small saucepan, bring milk and butter to a boil and then beat into mixture. Measure sifted flour, then sift together with the baking powder and beat into mixture. Pour mixture very quickly into greased and floured 8 X 8 inch pan. Bake for 25-30 minutes. This is a fine grain cake. Makes 16 servings.

Laurel

Laurel V. Haseley

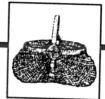

CHOCOLATE CAKE

1	16 ounce can Hershey's syrup
4	whole eggs
1	cup cake flour
1	cup granulated sugar
½	cup butter
	powdered sugar

Preheat oven to 350°F. In a large bowl, cream sugar and butter. Add eggs, syrup and flour; blend well. Grease large tube pan and line with waxed paper. Spoon batter into pan and bake for 45 minutes. Let cool in pan. Invert onto serving platter. Sprinkle top of cake with powdered sugar.

Kay

Kay English

From an old boyfriend's mother - it did not win his heart...

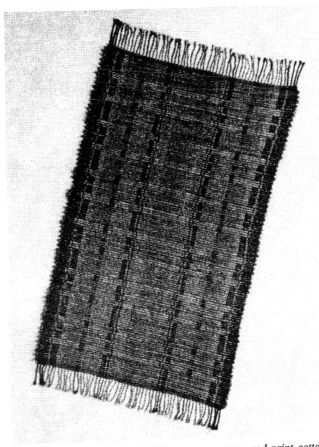

Gloria B. Skovronsky, 62" X 39", rag rug, cotton and print cotton fabrics, woven in log cabin, 1991.

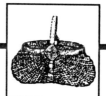

SANDTORTE (Gloria's Bundt Cake)

1	cup soft butter (no substitute)
3	cups granulated sugar
6	whole eggs
1	cup commercial sour cream
3	cups all-purpose flour, sifted
¼	teaspoon baking powder
1½	teaspoons vanilla
	powdered sugar, sifted

Preheat oven to 350°F. In large bowl, cream butter and blend in sugar. Add eggs, one at a time, beating well after each. Blend in sour cream. Measure sifted flour and sift together with baking powder. Add flour mixture in 4-5 equal parts to first mixture, blending well. Add vanilla. Spoon batter into well buttered 2-2½ quart mold or into 9 inch tube pan. Bake about 1 hour 20 minutes (watch last few minutes carefully) or until it tests done with a toothpick. When done, let stand for 5 minutes, then invert on cooling rack. Cool completely, then wrap tightly in plastic or foil and leave for 24 hours at room temperature before serving. Before slicing into wedges, sprinkle the top with sifted powdered sugar. Makes about 16 servings.

Gloria

Gloria B. Skovronsky

My mom had this recipe forever, and I think she got it from one of the Danish women in the family. Mom only made it as a special dessert and, although you were supposed to wait 24 hours before cutting it, the cake never lasted that long. Excellent for a buffet, because you can dress it up if you like, and it serves a lot of people.

163

POPPY SEED CAKE

1	18¼ ounce package lemon supreme cake mix
1	3 ounce package lemon Jello
1	3 ounce package lemon instant pudding mix
3	tablespoons poppy seeds (1 is often enough)
1¼	cups cold water
½	cup cooking oil
4	whole eggs

Glaze:
> juice of 1 lemon

1/3   cup granulated sugar

Preheat oven to 350°F. Mix cake mix, Jello, pudding mix and poppy seeds together in large bowl. Make a deep well in center and add water, oil and eggs. Beat for four minutes on low-medium speed with electric mixer. Pour into well-greased and floured 12 inch bundt pan (9 X 13 inch pan may be used but watch timing). Bake for 50-60 minutes or until cake tests done with toothpick. Let cake cool. Remove cake from pan and blend the lemon juice and sugar to drizzle on top. Makes 12 servings.

Clara

Clara Mitchell

This is a very old recipe. Everyone raves about its lemony moistness.

WEAVING PEGGY'S CHEESECAKE

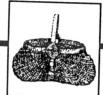

Crumb crust:
12-14   graham crackers, crumbled
2   tablespoons granulated sugar
3   tablespoons butter, melted
Filling:
4   egg whites, whipped
1   cup granulated sugar
3   8 ounce packages cream cheese, room
         temperature
3   tablespoons light rum (can melt with 4 ounces
         bittersweet chocolate)
Topping:
2   cups sour cream
2   tablespoons granulated sugar

Preheat oven to 350°F. Mix the crackers, sugar and melted butter and press into an 8-9 inch springform pan. In a large bowl whip egg whites until stiff, gradually adding sugar to make meringue. Cream the cream cheese and rum together in large bowl until smooth. Fold meringue gently into cheese mixture. Pour onto crust. Bake for 45 minutes. Remove cake from oven and cool. Raise oven temperature to 450°F. Blend sour cream and sugar together and pour over cooled cake. Bake for 5 minutes. Makes 12 servings.

Caroline Jorstad

I don't know who Peggy was - a voice "looming" from the past, perhaps, but I have used this recipe for years in spite all of the alarm about cholesterol. Now, you could use light cream cheese and yoghurt, BUT it won't be Weaving Peggy's.

WHITE CHOCOLATE BERRY CHEESECAKE

Crust:
1¼	cup chocolate wafer cookies (3/4 package Nabisco brand), finely ground
¼	cup almonds, ground (about 1 ounce)
2	tablespoons granulated sugar
1/8	teaspoon almond extract
3	tablespoons (or more) unsalted butter, melted

Filling:
6	ounces white chocolate, imported, finely chopped
3	8 ounce packages cream cheese, room temperature
8	ounces Neufchatel cheese, room temperature - may substitute with 6 ounces mixed berry or strawberry Neufchatel cheese (check your local supermarket deli) plus 2 ounces plain Neufchatel cheese
5	large whole eggs, room temperature
3/4	cup granulated sugar
3	tablespoons all-purpose flour
1	teaspoon vanilla extract
¼	teaspoon almond extract

Glaze:
7	tablespoons whipping cream
8	ounces white chocolate (as described in filling)

Topping:
1	8 ounce carton strawberries or raspberries, frozen, thawed, pureed and strained
	marzipan paste

166

WHITE CHOCOLATE BERRY
CHEESECAKE, cont'd.

Preheat oven to 350°F. To make the crust: In a small bowl mix, cookie crumbs, almonds, sugar, almond extract. Blend in enough butter to bind crumbs. Press mixture firmly into bottom of 10 inch springform pan. Bake 10 minutes. Cool completely.

Reduce oven heat to 325°F. To make filling: Melt chocolate in double boiler over simmering water stirring until smooth. Cool to lukewarm. Using an electric beater, beat cheeses until smooth. Blend in eggs one at a time. Mix in sugar, flour, vanilla and almond extract. Stir 1 cup cheese mixture into lukewarm white chocolate, then mix into remaining filling. Pour filling over crust. Bake until cheesecake is firm around edges, but still moves slightly in center when pan is shaken, about 40 minutes. Transfer to a rack and cool completely. Cover and refrigerate overnight.

To make glaze: Bring cream to simmer in heavy saucepan over low heat. Add chocolate and stir until smooth. Spoon glaze over top of cheesecake. Using a spatula, spread glaze slightly over edge. Refrigerate until glaze is set.

To make topping: Blend some marzipan with the fruit puree to make a thick paste. Swirl or dribble decoratively on top. Refrigerate. (Cheesecake may be prepared 2 days ahead.) Makes 12 servings.

Valerie

Valerie L. Day

This is a very rich cheesecake!!

ALICE'S FABULOUS NOODLE KUGEL

8   ounces broad egg noodles
3   whole eggs
½   cup granulated sugar
1   cup sour cream
1   cup cottage cheese
3/4 cup whole milk
1   16 ounce can fruit of your choice, drained
2   tablespoons butter, melted
1   teaspoon vanilla
     cinnamon (optional)

Preheat oven to 350°F. Place noodles in boiling water and cook 10 minutes; drain. In large bowl, beat eggs and sugar. Blend in sour cream, cottage cheese, milk, fruit, butter and vanilla. Add noodles and mix well. Turn into greased 2 quart 9 X 13 inch baking casserole. Sprinkle with cinnamon, if desired. Bake 1 hour. Serve hot or cold.

Sari

Sari Susan Kaplan

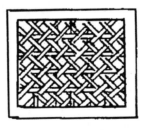

plaiting

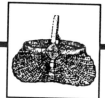

CLAFOUTI

1¼	cups 1% milk
3	whole eggs
2	teaspoons vanilla extract
¼	cup granulated sugar
2/3	cup all-purpose flour
¼	teaspoon salt
2	cups of fresh Washington bing cherries, pitted
	powdered sugar

Preheat oven to 350°F. Blend milk, eggs and vanilla in food processor for 1 minute. Add sugar and blend. Add flour and salt; mix 1 minute. Pour ¼ inch layer of batter in Pyrex pie pan. Set over moderate heat for 1-2 minutes until a film of batter has set in the bottom of the dish. Remove from heat. Spread cherries over the batter. Pour on the rest of the batter and smooth the surface. Bake for 1 hour or until it has puffed and browned and a knife inserted comes out clean. Sprinkle with powdered sugar. Serve warm. Makes 6-8 servings.

Evelyn

Evelyn B. Tuller

One morning at our San Juan Island Bed and Breakfast -- Moon & Sixpence -- I served this Clafouti. It's a traditional French peasant dessert from the "Limousin" but I cut the amount of sugar and serve it at breakfast. One of our guests was a World War II war bride from France. As she tasted this dish she exclaimed, "Clafouti! Where did you get the recipe?" She shared that the only times she had eaten Clafouti in her 40+ years of living in the U.S. was when she or her daughter made it. How this French recipe became part of my Pennsylvania Dutch kitchen repertoire is another story.

Sue Ewens, Nantucket basket, 10" x 9" x 7", woven with black ash and reed with white oak handles, 1991.

APPLE CRISP

4 cups apples, peeled and sliced
½ cup water
1 teaspoon cinnamon

Topping:
1 cup sugar
3/4 cup all-purpose flour
½ cup butter or margarine

Preheat oven to 375°F. Place apples in buttered shallow casserole dish; add water and cinnamon. In small mixing bowl, add sugar and flour. Cut butter into mixture and spread evenly on top of apples. Bake for 40-50 minutes. Makes 4 servings.

Alene

Alene Patterson

This recipe has been in our family for three generations. It came from my grandmother, Anna Arndt Fenske, who lived in Oconto, Wisconsin.

market basket

BANANAS FLAMBÉ

1   tablespoon butter
2   tablespoons brown sugar, packed
1   ripe banana, peeled, sliced lengthwise
      or diagonally
½   ounce orange flavored liqueur
1   ounce dark rum
      vanilla ice cream

For each individual serving: Melt butter and sugar in a flat chafing dish. Add banana; sauté until tender. Pour in liqueur and rum over all and light with match to flame. (If you have difficulty getting it to flame, place liqueurs in a stainless steel spoon which has been heated over a flame.) Baste bananas with warm liquid until flame burns out. Serve immediately over vanilla ice cream.

Melba

Melba Short

For a dramatic finish to a dinner party, the busy hostess (and what weaver isn't always busy?) can serve this easy and tasty dessert. Once in Hawaii, I was asked to make it for a potluck. Unable to find the more usual Cointreau or Triple Sec in miniature, we found Grand Marnier. The substitution was a raving success!

CRUNCHY GRANOLA

4   cups uncooked oats, old fashioned
1   cup wheat germ
1   cup raw oat bran
1   cup almonds, slivered (or peanuts)
¼   cup sesame seeds
¼   cup rye flour
3/4 teaspoon salt
1   teaspoon vanilla
3/4 cup corn oil
3/4 cup honey (or molasses or brown sugar)

Preheat oven to 325°F. In a roasting pan, mix oats, wheat germ, oat bran, nuts, sesame seeds, flour and salt. In small sauce pan, heat together the vanilla, corn oil and honey. Pour liquid mixture over dry ingredients and mix well with large spoon. Bake 10-15 minutes. Stir occasionally while cooling. Serve as a morning cereal or eat as a snack. Dried fruit can be added when served.

Murph

Murph Shapley

My friend, Jean Parker, got this recipe heaven knows where. I have modified it to my preference. It's my favorite cereal snack.

cat's head basket

173

APPLE TORTE

Crust:
½ cup butter
1/3 cup granulated sugar
¼ teaspoon vanilla
1   cup all-purpose flour
Filling:
1 8 ounce package cream cheese, softened
¼ cup granulated sugar
1   whole egg
½ teaspoon vanilla
¼ teaspoon almond extract
Topping:
4   cups apples, peeled, thinly sliced
½ teaspoon cinnamon
¼ cup raisins
1/3 cup granulated sugar
1   teaspoon lemon juice

Preheat oven to 450°F. In medium bowl, cream butter and sugar; add vanilla and flour. Mix well and spread on bottom and side of an 8½ inch springform pan. In a bowl, combine softened cream cheese, sugar and egg and beat on medium speed until smooth and creamy. Spread over pastry crust. Toss apples with cinnamon, raisins, sugar and lemon juice. Spoon over cream cheese layer. Bake 10 minutes at 450°F, then reduce heat to 400°F and bake 25 minutes more, or until apples are the desired tenderness and crust is light brown. Chill in pan 8 hours before serving. Unspring sides and place on serving dish. Makes 8 servings.

Linda

Linda C. Smith

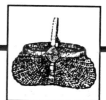

DANISH PASTRY

Crust:
1 cup all-purpose flour
½ cup butter
2 tablespoons cold water

Filling:
1 cup water
½ cup butter
1 cup all-purpose flour
1 tablespoon almond extract
3 whole eggs

Icing:
3/4 cup powdered sugar
2 teaspoons milk
¼ teaspoon almond extract
almonds, sliced

Preheat oven to 350°F. Cut butter into flour until it resembles a coarse meal. Add cold water and mix with fork until a ball of dough forms. (This can also be done in a food processor.) Divide dough in half. Makes two 3 X 12 inch strips. Place on greased cookie sheet. Bring water and butter to a boil. Add flour and beat until a stiff ball forms. Add flavorings and eggs, one at a time, beating well. Spread the filling over the crust. Bake 1 hour. Cool. Mix powdered sugar, milk and almond extract. Drizzle over pastry and top with almonds. Makes 2 pastries.

Linda Jaeger

TRIFLE

1   package pound cake, sponge fingers or any
     leftover cake, cut into 2 inch cubes
     sherry to flavor (optional)
1   6 ounce package strawberry or raspberry Jello,
     prepared according to instructions - DO NOT
     LET SET
1   large package instant vanilla pudding mix,
     prepared according to instructions (or make
     your own custard)
1   can mandarin oranges (or other fruit)
1   cup whipping cream, whipped

Optional:
½ cup sherry poured over the cake to taste
    chopped walnuts or coconut shreds for garnish

Place cake cubes on bottom and sides of a glass bowl. Pour sherry over cubes if desired. Arrange the orange slices or other fruit over the cake attractively. Gently pour the cooled, but not set, Jello over the cake. Refrigerate. When set, add the prepared pudding or custard as the second layer. Just before serving, top with whipped cream. Garnish as desired.

Irene

Irene Ohannesian

Trifle is an often used recipe in England and reminds me of my childhood. It began as a means of using up stale cake. It can be simple or "fancy" and no two trifles ever taste alike. Some variations are to use chocolate cake or chocolate swirled into the pudding.

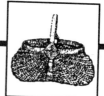

SHRIKARD

2 cups sour cream
1 cup granulated sugar
¼ teaspoon fresh ground cardamom
1 cup salted cashews

Put sour cream into a cheesecloth bag and let drain over a bowl overnight. Discard liquids. Add cardamom and sugar to curds and blend. Place in mound on glass plate and cover with nuts. Serve with fresh fruits.

Murph

Murph Shapley

Originally, this recipe came from a memoir of living in India, author unknown. My family has loved it for almost 40 years, particularly with strawberries. At my son's wedding, the caterer, who had lived in India, produced a variation that used almonds and a bit of rose water. Recently, I've tried making it with yoghurt, low fat yoghurt and finally no fat yoghurt. All three worked just fine and there is an added dividend because yoghurt "cheese" only takes 4 hours to drip. It then makes a marvelous low calorie base for all kinds of dips.

coiled basket

Jan Paul, pillow, 18" x 12", deersuede, woven in double corduroy technique, 1987.

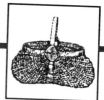

PERSIMMON PUDDING

1   cup granulated sugar
1   cup all-purpose flour
1   teaspoon baking soda
½   teaspoon salt
1   teaspoon ground cinnamon
1   whole egg
¼   cup milk
1   cup persimmon pulp
1   teaspoon vanilla
1   teaspoon butter, melted
1   cup nuts, chopped
1   cup raisins

Preheat oven to 350°F. Grease and line a 9 X 5 X 3 inch loaf pan. Line sides and bottom of greased pan with waxed paper. Mix sugar, flour, soda, salt, cinnamon, egg, milk, persimmon, vanilla, butter, nuts and raisins together until well blended. Spoon mixture into prepared loaf pan. Bake for 1 hour. Makes 1 loaf.

Jan

Jan Paul

My parents were given this recipe when they were married 55 years ago. It is wonderful to serve during the holiday season and makes unusual hostess gifts. The consistency is more that of a very moist bread, rather than a pudding.

APLETS

2 cups thick homemade unsweetened applesauce
    (bottled applesauce is too thin and sweet)
2 cups granulated sugar
2 tablespoons plain gelatin
6 tablespoons cold water
1 tablespoon squeezed lemon juice
1 cup nut meats of your choice, broken
    powdered sugar to dust
    cornstarch to dust

To make applesauce: Peel apples and place in large stock pot. Don't add water unless it starts sticking. Place lid to cover with very low heat. Stir occasionally. When cooked down to mush, sieve in ricer or grinder. Cook again if too thick.

To make aplets: Add sugar to applesauce and cook slowly for half an hour until very thick. While this is cooking, dissolve gelatin in the water and soak. While apples are still hot, stir into the gelatin. Cool and add lemon juice and nut meats. Spread into 9 X 13 inch baking dish and let set for 2 hours or until firm. Cut into bars and roll in powdered sugar and cornstarch mixture. Set in a warm place for two days and roll again. Repeat this until they are no longer sticky. Makes about 60 bars.

Betty

Betty Hagedorn

180

APLETS

2	tablespoons Knox gelatin
1¼	cups unsweetened applesauce, homemade
2	cups granulated sugar
2	teaspoons vanilla
1	cup nuts, chopped
	powdered sugar

Soak the gelatin in 3/4 cup applesauce for 10 minutes. Mix the sugar with the remaining 3/4 cup applesauce. Bring to boil, stirring constantly. Stir in nuts and vanilla. Pour into shallow, greased pan and let set 24 hours. Cut into small pieces and roll in powdered sugar.

To make homemade applesauce: Cook the sliced apples with the tiniest amount of water possible (I now use the microwave). Keep stirring while cooking. The gelatin must be mixed with cold applesauce. Timing seems important, so I let the gelatin mixture stand 5-6 minutes before putting the sugar and sauce mixture on to boil.

Jan

Jan Paul

My former Mother-in-Law gave me this recipe in the late 1950s. She had made it for years before that. King apples make a good tasting aplet, but be sure the applesauce is cold before you start to make this recipe.

EASY ICE CREAM "2-2-2"

2 quarts milk
2 cans sweetened condensed milk
2 teaspoons vanilla

Add the milks and vanilla together into ice cream freezer (hand crank or electric). Follow freezer instructions on making ice cream.

Option: Add fruits, chocolate or other flavorings of your choice.

Eat heartily and enjoy!

Marilyn

Marilyn Bomgren

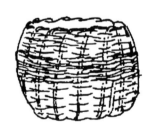

twined basket

DAISY CREAM CANDY

3   cups granulated sugar
1   cup water
1/3 cups butter
1   drop food coloring
2   teaspoons flavoring of your choice

In a medium sauce pan, mix sugar, water, butter and coloring; at low temperature slowly bring to 260° on a candy thermometer. Butter large area on a heat-proof counter or marble slab and pour thinly over area very fast. Add flavoring and with buttered hands gather candy and pull until it's opaque. Lift up and pull into a rope then cut in lengths of your choice. Let it stand until creamy, then store in a tight container.

Isabel

Isabel Inman

Anita Peckham was a well-known and much loved teacher of weaving and spinning in the Seattle area. She was also a noted pianist, a leather and wood-worker and a gourmet cook. Anita gave me this recipe around 1978.

Index of Contributors

PEANUT BUTTER PUBLISHING
Elliot Wolf, Publisher
200 Second Avenue West
Seattle, WA 98119
  (206) 281-5965

PHOTOGRAPHY for ARTISTS AND ILLUSTRATORS
William Wickett
540 First Avenue South
Suite 201
Seattle, WA 98104
  (206) 622-5537

ILLUSTRATOR
Nancy Nelson
21211 Northeast 13th Court
Redmond, WA 98053
  (206) 868-2144

GRAPHICS
Molly Petram
321 214th Avenue Northeast
Redmond, WA 9853
  (206) 391-3464

NORTHWEST MANNEQUIN
Joe Miller
9520 Sixth Avenue Northwest
Seattle, WA 98177
  (206) 783-8084

THE WEAVING WORKS
4717 Brooklyn Avenue Northeast
Seattle, WA 98105
  (206) 524-1221

COTTAGE WEAVING
485 Front Street North
Issaquah, WA 98027
  (206) 392-3492

SEATTLE WEAVERS' GUILD
P.O. Box 1153
Woodinville, WA 98072

Thrum Notes. . .

Thrum Notes. . .

ORDER FORM

To order additional copies of **Thrums From Weavers' Kitchens, A Cookbook from the Seattle Weavers' Guild**, send $11.95 plus postage and handling of $2.50 for one copy (75¢ for each additional copy) to:

Seattle Weavers' Guild
P.O. Box 1153
Woodinville, WA 98072

Name _____

Address _____

City, State, Zip _____

_____ copies @ $11.95 each _____

8.2% sales tax _____
(WA residents only)

shipping and handling _____

TOTAL _____

Wholesale discounts available.
Please inquire.